GROW YOUR OWN FOOD

To Maris Rea, NDH CDH
who has been a loyal friend for very many years

GROW YOUR OWN FOOD

Dr. W. E. Shewell-Cooper

Adam and Charles Black · London

First published 1976 by
Adam and Charles Black
35 Bedford Row, London WC1R 4JH

ISBN 0 7136 1622 9

Filmset and printed in Great Britain by
BAS Printers Limited, Wallop, Hampshire

by the same author

The Royal Gardeners
Flowers in Colour
The Garden
The Horticultural Note-Book
The Gardeners' Standby
The Reason Why of Gardening
Cook what you Grow
Continuous Flower Growing
The Complete Gardener
The Scout's Book of Gardening
The Women's Land Army Handbook
Modern Flower Growing for Profit
Modern Market Gardening
Modern Glasshouse Flowers for Profit
Born Gardeners
Enjoy your Gardening
The Complete Vegetable Grower
The Rhododendron Pocket Book
The Chrysanthemum Pocket Book
Children's Gardening Book
The Fundamentals of Alpine Gardening
Your Weekends in the Garden
George, Market Gardener
The Fundamentals of Gardening
Mini-work Gardening
The Complete Fruit Grower
Town and City Gardening
The Semi-detached Garden
The Beginners' Guide to Pot Plants
Cut Flowers for the Home
Tomatoes, Salads and Herbs
The Basic Book of Vegetables
The Basic Book of Flowers
The Basic Book of Rock Gardens and Pools
The Basic Book of Flowering Shrubs
The Basic Book of Chrysanthemums

The Basic Book of Roses
The Basic Book of Pruning
The Basic Book of Cloches and Frames
The Complete Greenhouse Gardener
Compost Gardening
The Guide to Soil, Humus and Health
Growing and Cooking Vegetables the Natural Way

Contents

Illustrations

1 The necessity for growing your own food

It makes all the difference in the world to have your own fresh vegetables, salads and fruits. First of all home grown vegetables – especially when compost grown – taste far better, and are richer in vitamins than those that have been produced in a market garden and sent first to market and then to the shop where they may have 'sat' for three or four days. Fresh vegetables and salads are better than stale ones.

Then there is always the danger that the market gardener has sprayed his crops with, say, D.D.T. and though there may be only a slight deposit on the vegetables this can build up in the body of human beings to serious proportions. In the experiments carried out at the research centre of *The Good Gardeners' Association* at Arkley Manor, it has been shown that the compost grown vegetables are less 'acid', and have far better flavour than those grown with chemical fertilizers, and such fertilizers are invariably used by large scale market gardeners.

There is also a question of cost. Vegetables these days tend to be expensive. It is far far cheaper to grow your own, and even in small gardens some vegetables can be produced. In the Arkley Research Centre it has been proved that it is quite possible to produce at least £200 worth of vegetables and salads in a piece of land 60 yards by 10 yards. This is at the price level of 1975 – and it may be that by 1977 onwards the savings will be very much greater. Supplying people with fresh food is one of the most important problems facing us today, and it is likely to increase in severity.

The man who grows his own food is always more independent than the man who does not. Even in normal times the distribution of vegetables and other perishable foodstuffs is a big problem. There are occasions when there are food gluts in one country and a scarcity in the big towns of another. The obvious thing is for each to grow as much food as possible, thereby doing the country a great service in helping it to be self-supporting.

The degree of freshness in vegetables also makes a great deal of difference to how palatable they are. There is far less wastage when the vegetable is cut or dug up and used immediately than when it has to be packed, marketed and transported.

One's own garden may seem too small to be of much use to the nation. Yet the millions of small gardens all over the country make up tens of thousands of acres, which, if used properly, can produce thousands of tons of food. Even the man in the flat can set out to have an allotment. Everyone can do their bit. Children, too, often show grown-ups what can be done as is demonstrated by many school garden plots.

This book, therefore, is designed to help everyone. It caters for the small and large garden. It deals with the most important crops – the most valuable crops. It has been written without superfluous detail; urgency has been the theme throughout every chapter.

It is hoped that this book will be the means of encouraging thousands all over the country to 'grow more'.

[*The Good Gardeners' Association* can be of great value to food growers who value the free advice given to members by post or phone. Anyone can become a Fellow on payment of £3 a year. Write to the General Secretary, The Good Gardeners' Association, Arkley Manor, Arkley, Nr. Barnet, Herts.]

2 The importance of making your own compost

It has been a great pleasure during the last twenty-four years to have played a part in the conversion of a considerable number of gardens all over the world into organic gardens. There is ample evidence as to the improvement both in growth and flavour of vegetables and fruit.

The first thing to do is to establish at least two (if not a series) of compost bins. The moment one is full and is capped with soil, the next one should be filled. Make the bin with wooden sides with an inch or so of space between the planking. Generally speaking a bin 4 ft by 4 ft will do; but with the larger country garden, I advise the making of 8 ft by 8 ft bins. (In the gardens of *The Good Gardeners' Association* there are five bins, each 10 ft by 10 ft.)

When the bins have been erected side by side – preferably in a shady part of the garden and with a level earth floor, start collecting all the organic matter week by week so as to fill bin no. 1. Anything that has lived can go on the heap. It is surprising what comes under this heading, the tops of peas and beans, potatoes, beetroot, carrots, lawn mowings, the stumps of the brassicas (bash them up on a chopping block with an axe), the refuse from the kitchen – tea leaves, coffee grounds, fluff from the Hoover, fish bones, and even old newspapers after they have been soaked in water. Cotton and worn out woollens, leaves, and even straw when it is available can also be added.

The moment there is a 6 inch thickness of whatever you are collecting, apply what is called the activator, that is a good fish manure, seaweed manure, dry poultry manure or rabbit manure at 3 ozs to the square yard. If the organic material is very dry, water it – but if it is damp like lawn mowings, don't. Eventually the heap will rise to a height of, say, 7 ft. Then you should cap it with 2 inches of soil – like the crust of a cake – in order to keep in the moisture. Then start on bin no. 2 while bin no. 1 is rotting down and forming the nice, brown, powdery compost which should be ready in six months time.

Traditional usage says the compost should be dug or forked in. The organic method is to put the compost on the top of the earth in November and let the worms pull in what is needed to build up the humus content of the soil. It may sound quite wrong to avoid digging, but the author hasn't dug his vegetable gardens for fourteen years and gets magnificent results.

When a novice starts gardening and has not been able to make sufficient compost to use in this way, then sedge peat should be used instead. This is a vital substitute for compost, *not* sphagnum peat or moss peat, but 'live' sedge peat – medium grade is best. The compost, of course, costs little whereas sedge peat may be expensive.

So, the ideal way of growing healthy delicious vegetables is not to dig, but to put the layer of compost 1 inch deep all over the land. Then in the spring when the seed has to be sown, what is left of the compost is raked in to the top inch or so of soil.

Gardeners who use the sedge peat mulching idea in the vegetable garden, should know that it takes about 10 cwt to cover 100 square yards about 1 inch deep. The plan is to sow the seeds in the spring on the surface of the ground and then to cover with peat. The result is that there is no necessity for weeding at all, and the mulch created ensures very heavy crops even in dry weather. There is nothing better than sedge peat or compost for keeping the moisture in the ground. The peat has to be replaced each autumn but at the end of six years there's usually sufficient organic matter present in the ground for another three or four years. The plan is to scratch a little drill in the compost or sedge peat and sow the seeds in the normal way, following this with a light raking to cover.

There is no doubt that the placing of fine organic matter on the surface of the soil does give tremendous encouragement to the worms. They get busy pulling the surface material into the soil, and thus they are working up and down continuously, providing natural channels down which the moisture can percolate and the air can go. The worms really do the digging for you; in the right way and at the right time. This is particularly useful in heavy soils, for clays are wonderfully improved when man's friend, the worm, is allowed to do the work day by day.

Those who have been gardening on fully organic lines for some years are seldom bothered, I find, by pests and diseases, a sure indication that they are providing healthy conditions for plants. It would be too much to expect complete immunity, perhaps.

To sum up then: the gardener who is keen to turn over his land to a fully organic garden must do it by the addition of plenty of organic matter and by suppressing weeds in the proper way. He must make all the compost possible, but during the first two or three years, while he is building up the humus content of the soil, he may have to buy inorganic matter in the form of sedge peat. His whole object is to build up the humus content of the soil, for when this is done the millions of living organisms in the soil will do the rest. Remember there are more than twenty-eight living beneficial organisms in a handful of soil. It is these god-given creatures that will keep the plants growing heathily and they do not ask for any chemical fertilizers at all.

At the research centre of *The Good Gardeners' Association* at Arkley, no chemical fertilizers have been used for fifteen years. In addition, no digging, forking or hoeing has been done during this period. The powdery compost is put all over the soil 1 inch deep, and there are no annual weeds at all.

Note that the two rules in respect of compost vegetable growing are:

1 Everything that has lived can live again in another plant, and
2 Only a plant *really knows* what another plant needs.

It will be a relief to those who are taking up food production to know that the Rothamstead Experimental Station has shown that deep cultivation (digging and forking) is by no means necessary for the production of good crops.

DIGGING AND BASTARD TRENCHING

For those, therefore, who *cannot* contemplate gardening without digging, the following instructions are given on 'bastard trenching'. This is a method of incorporating organic manures into the soil. A trench 2 ft wide and a spade's depth is dug out at one end of the plot. The soil from this trench is then taken to the other end of the plot (or the plot may be divided up into two portions, as in the diagram on page 7, and the soil from A is then deposited at D. It is necessary then to walk from A to B and from C to D, putting the top soil from the end of C to the bottom of B, and finding the soil to fill the last trench at D.

When trench A has been made, the gardener should get down into the trench and fork it over lightly. He should work methodically from one end to the other. The compost should be forked in at the same time, and another layer of well-rotted compost can then be put on top, and so appears as the 'meat in the sandwich', as seen in the diagram on page 7.

The soil from A1 is put into the trench A on top of the manure, and when this is done the gardener gets into the bottom of trench A1, treats this in the same way as trench A, and covers it with the soil from A2. He works like this right the way down the plot, leaving the soil rough as he does so.

This digging is best carried out in the autumn, when the clods of soil should be left lumpy, so that they may be acted on by the frosts and winds.

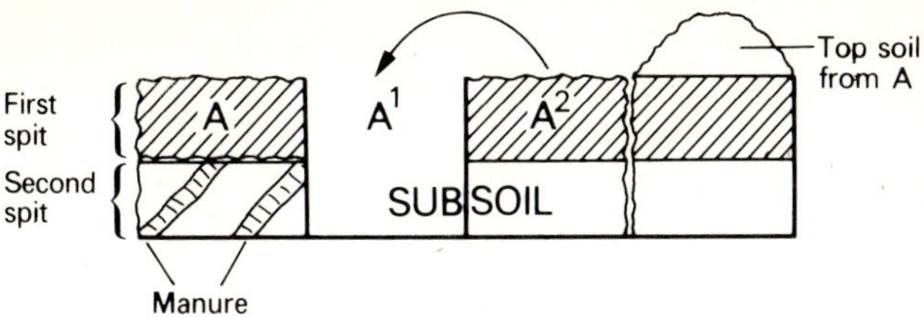

Double digging

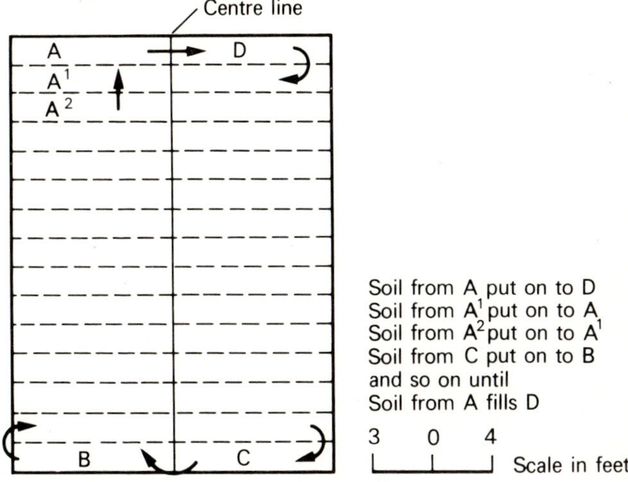

The method of digging an allotment

FORKING

Before seeds are sown it is necessary to get 1 or 2 ins of the surface soil down to a fine tilth (a tilth is when every particle of soil in the top inch or so is no larger than a grain of wheat). It is impossible to produce a fine tilth if the soil is sticky and wet, and the best time to do this, therefore, is when the soil is just drying out but before it is too dry.

The operations usually adopted for getting the soil down to a fine tilth are those of forking and treading.

In stony soil there is no need to rake away every single stone that appears, for as a matter of fact, a certain number of surface stones are useful, in that they help to keep the soil moist underneath.

HOEING

Hoeing is an operation that every gardener must learn to do. It never does ground any harm to hoe out the weeds when it is not too wet. Keep a loose surface 1 inch of soil, and it will be found that the soil below is moist, and furthermore, that the weeds will be kept down. With the organic method, hardly any hoeing proves necessary.

The Dutch hoe is perhaps the best tool, and should be used while walking backwards. This way, the operator's footmarks are covered up. The hoe should not be driven deeply into the ground, for only ½ an inch of loose surface is required.

Draw-hoes are useful for thinning out seedlings.

MULCHING OR TOP-DRESSING

Reference has already been made to what is known as a dust mulch. This is a loose surface of dusty soil about ½ an inch deep which prevents the evaporation of the soil moisture below. Organic materials, such as sedge peat, very old manure, crushed bark from trees, or compost are more beneficial and can be used along the rows of plants all over the ground. If the roots of runner beans and peas are kept cool, for example, heavier crops result. These mulches add organic matter to the ground and smother weeds at the same time.

What mulching does The sedge peat mulch is put evenly all over the bed. It is important to see that the bed is made absolutely level before the sedge peat is applied. When this is ensured, annual weed seeds cannot grow, so there will be virtually no hoeing to do, for the life of the bed concerned. *The Good Gardeners' Association* has a demonstration garden at Arkley Manor, where there are beds which have been mulched for seventeen years with great success as there are no annual weeds at all.

Treading a seed-bed with boards strapped to the feet

You cannot, of course, smother and prevent perennial weeds from growing by mulching with compost or sedge peat. So if you are unlucky enough to have a garden with thistles, nettles, docks, couch or twitch grass, ground elder and the like, you must get rid of these with a strong hormone weedkiller. It is necessary to start with a garden free of perennial weeds, and then to use the sedge peat or compost to control the annual weeds.

It must be remembered that every time a gardener hoes his soil he disturbs thousands of weed seeds that have been lying dormant. This happens inevitably when you dig or fork. Move soil and you disturb weed seeds that may have been lying there for many years and then they break into growth. The mulching scheme makes soil disturbance quite unnecessary.

3 The main essentials for growing food
Preparation and feeding the soil

THE IMPORTANCE OF CORRECT MANURING

The vegetable gardener should do everything possible to see that the soil that he cultivates is kept enriched with organic matter. The food value, the flavour, the quality of the vegetables and the vitamin content cannot be at a high level unless some properly made compost is applied in each season.

This organic matter assists in the aeration of the soil, and helps to produce a better mechanical and physical condition. It provides the humus which is all-important. Plants that are growing on land that has been enriched regularly with compost do not suffer as seriously from pests and diseases as plants growing on soil which is deficient in humus.

It is necessary, therefore, to add the organic compost and only to use in addition, if necessary, organic fertilizers like hoof and horn meal, fish manure or seaweed powder for rectifying any deficiencies there may be.

Fresh animal manure, when dug in, may have a harmful effect, and it is important, therefore, to see that it is really old before it is dug in. Well-rotted manure is always more valuable, though it is equally important to see that it is composted.

A good dressing of compost or old manure is one good barrow-load to 10 square yards.

Night Soil Human excreta is valuable, providing it is obtained from earth closets which today are rare. The solid matter that is left behind in cesspools and manure 'farms' is of little value, for the plant foods lie in the liquid portion. Town councils should be encouraged to compost sewerage wastes with dustbin waste, correctly, in order to be able to supply food producers with suitable powdery compost at a cheap rate.

Fish manure Fish manure is valuable, and is usually offered by the manufacturers free from any objectionable odour. It is an organic fertilizer that rots down rapidly and feeds the soil. It should be used at 4 ozs to the square yard. It is difficult to get in some years, but is usually obtainable from Maskells, Stephenson St, London.

Meat and bone meal and hoof and horn meal Two slow-acting manures which contain nitrogen and phosphates but no potash, and are usually forked into the top 3 or 4 ins of soil at 4 ozs to the square yard.

Hops Spent hops are quite a good substitute for compost, providing phosphates and potash are used in addition. They may be applied as a mulch or may be forked lightly in at the rate of 1 lb to the square yard.

Seaweed Those who live near the seaside should certainly use seaweed. When composted it is very valuable. It should be dug in in the autumn at the rate of one good barrow-load to 10 square yards or put on top of the soil in the same way as compost. The main interest of seaweed is not in its protein, carbohydrates or vitamins but in its mineral content, the most important trace mineral being iodine which is essential for the body.

Seaweed is also rich in potassium and magnesium and also contains all of the trace minerals that are important for human nutrition. Seaweeds are certainly not, of course, weeds as such but natural organic mineral storehouses. Seaweed can be used as an activator on the compost heap or may be composted on its own and applied like sedge peat as a top dressing.

Sedge peat Those who can get hold of sedge peat should use it. It can be forked in at the rate of 4 lbs to the square yard. Advice may be obtained beforehand from *The Good Gardeners' Association*, to whom enquiries should be addressed at Arkley Manor, Arkley, near Barnet, who offer a detailed leaflet on the subject.

Soot This helps to darken light soils, and so enable them to absorb and retain heat better. It contains nitrogen only. It is generally used as a top dressing in the spring, at the rate of 5 ozs to the square yard.

Green manuring Those who cannot make compost from any of the wastes mentioned previously may add organic matter to their soil by means of green manure. This is obtained by growing plants and digging them in long before they come to maturity. Mustard, rye or vetches are often used; the seed is sowed broadcast, and the plants that result are dug in two or three months later. Some gardeners sow all the seeds that they have over towards the end of the season and dig in all the plants that grow up *en masse* for green manure, after having bashed them about to bruise and break them.

It should be noted that ground to be green manured has to be given up to this system for at least three months.

Double green manuring Where land is full of perennial weeds and lacking in organic matter too, it should be dug in the early spring and the seed of tares should be sown broadcast at the rate of ½ oz to the square yard. In June the crop should be knocked down with the spade and fish manure applied at the rate of 3 ozs to the square yard. The material should be left for eight days after this, and should then be dug in shallowly. The surface of the soil should then be cultivated and sown with rye, this rye being dug in in October or November.

This system entails giving up the plot of land for a whole year and should only be adopted where the ground is so foul with perennial weeds that it would be impossible to grow any vegetable crops.

THE USE OF ARTIFICIAL FERTILIZERS

If perfect growth is to be obtained, there are three plant foods which need to be present in the soil: nitrogen, phosphates and potash, and organic fertilizers may be used as supplements. These must be supplied in the right proportions, and it is useless to apply one of the substances in excess in the hope that it will make up for the deficiency in another.

Nitrogen assists in building up the stems and the green leaves of the plant. When too much nitrogen is given, the plant's energies seem to be directed towards the production of leaves and rank shoots, with the result that its fruitfulness may be impaired. An over-nitrogened plant is soft and subject to insect pests and fungus diseases. Too much nitrogen delays ripening.

For those who dislike the use of chemicals, dried blood at 2 ozs to a square yard provides the nitrogen. Soot is also useful used at say 6 ozs to the square yard. For poultry manure see below under 'Complete fertilizers'.

For those who do not mind using chemical fertilizers it is possible to give sulphate of ammonia or nitrate of soda in 1 or 2 ozs to the square yard.

Phosphates play their part with the roots. Crops grown on soil deficient in phosphates may ripen ten days or so later than crops grown on soil containing phosphates. Phosphates help to produce that steady, firm, continuous growth that is most valuable.

For those who do not mind using artificial chemicals, superphosphate may be applied at 3 ozs to the square yard.

Organic gardeners, however, use bone meal at 4 ozs to the square yard instead.

Potash plays an important part in the production of firm, well-flavoured vegetables. It is needed by all plants, which are healthier and better for its application owing to the strong fibre which results. Potash helps to give better colour and a heavier weight of crop. Sandy soils are normally deficient in this plant food.

Organic gardeners, however, use wood ashes at 6 ozs to the square yard instead.

Those who do prefer chemicals, apply sulphate of potash at 2 ozs to the square yard.

COMPLETE FERTILIZERS

From the point of view of saving time and labour, there is a lot to be said for standardising the extra food given to the vegetable crops. Use, therefore, a fish manure which 'contains' nitrogen, phosphates and potash as well as many other minor elements which help to feed the plant. The alternative is to use a seaweed manure. Both these are applied at 3–4 ozs to the square yard. There are also hoof and horn meal plus wood ashes and meat and bone meal plus wood ashes.

Poultry manure, when dried, is useful, used at 3 ozs to the yard run, but wood ashes must be also applied at 3 ozs to the square yard. Alternatively the poultry manure may be used as a nitrogen dressing *only* at 2 ozs to the square yard.

Liquid manure It is possible to buy seaweed manure as a liquid under the name of Scottish Seaweed.* You dissolve $\frac{1}{8}$ oz (a teaspoonful) to a gallon of water. 4 gallons of diluted manure should be used for 30 yards of row.

Tomatoes can have a gallon per plant every ten days when half-grown in the summer.

LIME

Lime should be applied on the surface of the ground

* This is obtainable from Kaye McInnes, Seaweed Croft, Seddes, Nairn, Scotland.

after the other manures have been forked in. It is important, as it sweetens the soil and prevents it from being acid. It improves the texture and workability of heavy soils, adds calcium as a plant food and by helping to decompose humus and organic compounds, releases other plant foods.

Regular applications of lime help to keep at bay the club root disease. Lime is not important for potatoes and roots but it is for cabbages, peas and beans. It is usual to apply hydrated lime at 3 or 4 ozs to the square yard as a top dressing.

SHALL I HAVE MY SOIL ANALYSED?

Fellows of *The Good Gardeners' Association* have the facility of having their soil analysed or tested for lime. I have, however, been asked by gardeners, whether there is any truth in the statement made by some people that soil analysis is useless. It is for this reason that I want to pass on the following information.

Dr L. Leyton of the University of Oxford has said that 'The damning thing about soil analysis is that you cannot get a proper sample. You should really analyse the soil around the absorbent part of the roots, which may be 10 ft down.' He goes on, 'I don't think soil analyses are any use at all, except as a general indicator.'

Dr E. Milton at the Research Station at Haughley, Suffolk, has been able to show over the last twelve years that a number of firmly held old-fashioned beliefs are quite unfounded. It is not true, for instance, that one single ordinary soil analysis will tell what a soil needs, irrespective of the month in which the sample is taken. He has taken samples at exactly the same spots in land, month after month, throughout the year and has been able to show that there is a natural rise in such plant foods as nitrogen, phosphates and potash in the summer months, and a natural fall in the winter months. So, to know the real needs of a soil it is necessary to take samples every month for at least a year.

This is not the end of the story by any means. Some chemists who make soil analyses then tell you how much of each chemical fertilizer you ought to apply. It has, of course, been assumed that the minerals the chemical fertilizers contain are taken up and used by the plants. The Haughley Research Station has proved that this is not true. The large acreage at Haughley is divided into three big sections. One of these has no chemical fertilizers applied on it at all, and Dr Milton has been able to prove that the plants on this section take up more minerals than plants on the other sections do, despite all the chemical fertilizers that have been added.

It seems that the utilization of minerals by the plants and the action of individual fertilizers is quite different indeed from what I was told as a student. Another thing I was always taught was that if I provided more tons of food per acre, then I would automatically produce more food per acre, but Dr Milton has shown that even this is a fallacy. Cows, for instance, fed on food which has been given compost or manure only, consistently give more milk from a far smaller quantity of food. We need, therefore, a biological rather than a chemical approach to our soil feeding. Further, because of the analysis made of all crops grown under the three different sections at Haughley, it has been proved that the addition of fertilizers is not necessarily connected with fertility, so in fact, the word has more or less lost its meaning.

The chemist may analyse the soil and say the phosphate content is low. He may advise the application of so many ounces of superphosphate per square yard – when in fact the organisms will produce *all* the requirements in nature's own quiet way!

4 Growing the members of the cabbage family

Under this heading I include all those crops, such as Brussels sprouts, cauliflower, broccoli, savoys, kale, etc., which are so important to our diet. Fresh cabbage is rich in vitamins A, B1, B2 and very rich in vitamin C. All members of the cabbage family are perishable. It is, therefore, of great importance that they should be freshly grown in all the gardens and allotments throughout Great Britain.

All members of the cabbage family are subject to the club root disease, and it is advisable not to grow them on the same piece of land for more than one year. The ground for this family should be well limed if there is any tendency for it to be at all acid. 7 to 8 ozs of garden lime should be used per square yard, and this should be applied to the surface of the soil before the plants are put out.

BROCCOLI

This is a crop that should be grown only in districts where it is known to succeed well, such as the south-west. It is possible, by careful planning and sowing, to produce beautiful white curds of broccoli from the Michaelmas Day of one year to the middle of June the following year.

Soil and Manuring Broccoli prefer firm soil and should follow a crop that has been well manured. Light soils may have compost added at the rate of one large barrow-load to 10 square yards. It is after this that firming is necessary.

The organic manure to use is bone meal at 3 ozs to the square yard and wood ashes at 2 ozs to the square yard.

Those who believe in using artificial manures should apply superphosphate at 1½ ozs to the square yard, sulphate of potash at ½ oz per square yard, just before planting.

Seed-sowing The seed should be sown in drills ½ inch deep, the soil tilth being fine. Most varieties can be sown during the second week of April, though the sowing of the June varieties may be delayed until the middle of May. Protect seedlings by means of black cotton, strung from short pieces of bamboo. The seed rows should be 9 inches apart.

Thin the seedlings out early, to prevent them from becoming too long and lanky. Transplant some of the seedlings to other beds 4 inches square if desired.

Planting Plant after such crops as early potatoes, French beans or even early peas. Distances apart – 2 ft by 2 ft. Firm well after planting. Put plenty of water in the hole at planting time, should the weather be dry.

General cultivation Unless the soil is covered with compost, you will need to hoe regularly. If the winter is hard, the plants may be pushed over so that their heads incline to the north. If after this process the plants seem to flag, they should be given a good watering.

Harvesting The curds should be cut directly they are ready. If too many 'turn in' at a time, a leaf or two should be broken and put over the white heads. Another method of keeping them is to pull up the whole plant and hang it upside down in a shed.

Varieties *For autumn and winter use:* English Winter; Snow's Winter White; Knight's Protecting and St. Buryan. *For spring use:* English Winter; Leamington; Armado April and Armado May. *For late or summer use:* English Winter; Royal Oak; May Blossom; Armado Tardo and English Winter, Late Queen.

SPROUTING BROCCOLI

Sprouting broccoli should certainly be grown in a national emergency, for it is quite hardy, goes on producing those elongated flower-heads which are delicious to eat, and at the end of its season the leaves may be used also. By growing several varieties it should be possible to have plenty of greenstuff to cut at from late September till the beginning of April.

Seed-sowing The seed should be sown in April, as advised for broccoli.

Planting Put the plants out 2 ft square *when ready*, on any land available.

General cultivation Regular hoeing, unless the soil is covered with compost.

Harvesting Cut the flower-shoots when they are found to be growing out in the axils of the leaves. Cut to within two-thirds of their length, and as a result more shoots will be thrown out on the same little stem. Do not cut the main leaves until all the sprouting tips have been consumed. It is the most economical crop to grow.

Varieties Calabrese; Green Comet and Late Corona; Purple Sprouting; Early Purple Sprouting and White Sprouting. In the White Sprouting group the recommended varieties are: Early White Sprouting; White Sprouting and Late White Sprouting.

N.B. This vegetable has been proved to be one of the most valuable from the point of view of vitamins, etc., and should certainly be grown more.

BRUSSELS SPROUTS

These should not be grown by the beginner unless he has a good deal of land available. They like a long season of growth, and cannot be hurried. They can, however, produce heavy crops when properly treated.

Soil and manuring Sprouts seem to like deeply prepared land, and so bastard trenching is advised by some. After trenching, the ground should be made firm. Firmness cannot be over-emphasized so the author never digs.

A well-piled barrow-load of composted vegetable refuse should be applied to every 8 square yards and in addition, an organic fertilizer like fish manure, or seaweed manure at 3 ozs to the square yard. If the plants are not growing satisfactorily after they have been growing in their permanent position for some time old soot may be applied at 1 oz to the yard run. A further dressing may be given a fortnight later.

Seed-sowing The main sowing should be done early in April in a finely prepared seed-bed. The drills should be ½ inch deep, 9 ins apart, and the seeds should be sown thinly. The plants that arise should be transplanted 6 ins square in another border before they get 'leggy'.

Sowings can also be made in frames early in March, or in a sheltered border the previous year in August.

Plantings The plants should be put out 2½ ft square during May or early June.

It is most important to inter-crop between the rows, in order to make the utmost use of the ground, and so spinach, radish or lettuce should be sown in between.

General cultivation Hoe throughout the summer if necessary and only remove the large leaves of the plants as they begin to turn yellow. Keep a look-out for the blue fly or aphis, and dust vigorously with derris if any signs of them appear.

Harvesting To make the most of sprout-plants cut off the sprouts with a knife, leaving a short stalk on the main stem. Do not break them off. The little short sprout-stems will then throw out further open sprouts, giving a valuable second crop.

Cutting should be done systematically from the

bottom of the stem upwards.

Varieties King Arthur; Prince Askold; Stabilo; Continuity Early Half Tall and Irish Elegance.

CABBAGES

There are spring, summer and winter cabbages, apart from the savoys (which are dealt with under a separate heading). There should be no difficulty in keeping up a supply of this excellent vegetable all the year round.

Care should be taken to ensure that the club root disease is kept down and that caterpillars and flea-beetles are controlled.

Soil and manuring Cabbages will grow on almost any soil, providing the ground has been properly treated. Compost should be added at the rate of one large barrowload to 10 square yards. In addition, fish manure or seaweed manure should be supplied at 4 ozs to the square yard. During the growing season a further dressing may be applied at 1 oz to the yard run, as seems necessary. Where digging is not done the compost is laid on the surface of the soil and raked in with a deep tined rake.

A reminder should be given about lime, which should be applied to the surface of the ground before the plants are put out. Garden lime is usually used at from 5 to 7 ozs per square yard.

Seed-sowing For spring cabbage – those are the cabbages that are cut in April and May – the seed should be sown later in July. The seed bed should be prepared as for broccoli, the seed being sown in drills 9 ins apart and ½ inch deep. Sow the seed thinly and there is no need to transplant.

For summer cabbage the seed should be sown in March.

For winter cabbage also, March sowing is desirable, and a second sowing, if necessary, early in May.

Planting Spring cabbages should be planted after such crops as early potatoes, peas or beans, during the month of September. The plants should be 12 ins apart, with 18 ins between the rows.

Summer cabbage should be put out when the plants are ready and whenever the land is free – 18 ins by 18 ins.

Winter cabbage should be put out 2 ft by 2 ft.

General cultivation The spring cabbages should not be given any nitrogen in the autumn, or they become too soft to live through the winter. They should be given seaweed manure or fish manure in March at the rate of 2 ozs per yard run, to hurry them along.

Summer and winter cabbage are often put out during dry weather, and should be well-watered in.

In all cases the rows should be hoed regularly, except that the spring cabbage should not be hoed during the wet winter months.

Harvesting Cut the cabbages directly they are ready to use, but do not leave the stalks in the ground, or they will rot the land. Smashed up they can easily be rotted down, with seaweed manure, on the vegetable compost heap.

Varieties *Spring cabbage:* Durham early; beautiful dark green, hardy and of first-rate quality. Durham Elf; very compact habit and high quality medium-sized hearts. First Early Market No. 218; one of the best early cabbages, producing the largest cabbage in the quickest time.

Summer cabbage: Emerald Cross; large ball-headed, solid and smooth. Primata; very early with small to medium-sized hearts which are very firm. Greyhound; good sized, pointed hearts with broad base; are solid and weighty and ready to cut weeks before others planted at the same time. Wiam; dark green and solid, very valuable. Golden Acre Primo; very early, dwarf and compact ball-headed variety.

Winter cabbage: Winnigstadt; compact variety with

solid, well-shaped pointed hearts. Christmas Drumhead; dwarf compact, hardy and productive. Winter White; large round and very solid light green hearts can be stored in a cool airy shed and remain in perfect condition for many weeks.

CAULIFLOWER

Not perhaps one of the most important crops in an emergency, but one which is very popular. It is subject to the same pests and diseases as cabbages, and so should be protected against them.

Soil and manuring The soil should be forked and compost incorporated at the rate of one good barrow-load to 10 square yards. Just before planting out, an organic fertilizer should be added as advised for cabbages. Finally, lime should be applied to the surface of the ground. The alternative is to put the compost on top of the ground and let the worms pull it in.

Seed-sowing To get an unbroken supply of good white curds from early June to the end of December, it is necessary to sow seeds at various times of the year.

An autumn sowing is made late in August or early in September, and the plants thus raised are pricked out into frames 4 ins square, where they live throughout the winter, to be planted out early in April in a sheltered part of the garden. January and February sowings can be made in boxes in frames or greenhouse, and when the young seedlings come through, the plants are pricked out 4 ins apart into further frames. These plants are put out early in April. Another sowing is often made out of doors late in March or early in April, in rows 6 ins apart, the seedlings being thinned out to 3 ins apart in the rows, when they are well through. Still later sowing may be made late in April or early in May in a similar manner.

With all these sowings it is necessary to take the utmost care to keep down the club root disease, and precautions should also be taken against the cabbage-root maggot when planting out.

Planting The autumn sowings are often planted early in March in a sheltered position, 1 ft square.

For the later sowings the rows are usually 2 ft apart, the plants being 18 ins apart in the rows. For the late summer sowings the rows should be $2\frac{1}{2}$ ft apart, the cauliflowers being 2 ft apart in the rows. Plants should always be put out before they get too big (bigger than 6 ins), as in this way better crops result.

General cultivation Hoeing must be done regularly between the plants, and during the dry weather copious watering should be given in addition.

When the plants are producing their white curds, one or two of the inner leaves should be bent over the flower to prevent it from turning yellow.

Harvesting The curds should be cut as early in the morning as possible. If too many heads turn in together, the plants may be pulled up with soil attached to the roots and hung up in a shed, as advised for broccoli.

Varieties *Autumn sowing:* Dominant; well protected heads, pure white, good size and of first-class quality. All the year round; large milk-white heads.

January and February sowings: Snowcap; very late, producing perfect, solid white heads of excellent quality.

Spring sowings: Snow King; extremely early, solid, well-rounded pure white heads of good quality and very uniform. Mechelse Delta; closely knit white heads of wonderful quality. Alpha; good medium sized heads of close white curds of finest quality. Snowball, Early Snowball; beautifully close white heads, small to medium size.

Later sowings: Flora Blanca; early September; solid white heads of exceptionally good quality. Flora Blanca, Torina; this grand new cauliflower is ready for cutting from September to December. Flora Blanca, Algromajo

No. 2; of enormous size and finest quality.

KALE

The kales are invaluable in an emergency, for they ensure a good supply of green vegetables, throughout the winter months. Instead of being harmed, they are improved by frosts.

Soil and manuring There is no need to make special preparations for kales, as they should follow another crop. If this is impossible, they may be manured as advised for cabbage.

Seed-sowing Seed-sowing is done the first week in March in the south and towards the end of March in the north.

A fine seed-bed should be prepared by raking down the soil well, in an open situation. The drills should be 9 ins apart, and if the plants have to be thinned and transplanted, they should be put out 6 ins square.

Asparagus kale seed may be sown as late as June and July.

Planting The plants should be ready to put out into their permanent positions at the end of June or the beginning of July. They are a useful crop to follow early potatoes, early peas, lettuce, spinach or French beans.

General cultivation See that the plants have plenty of water to start with. If dry, pour water in the holes at planting time. Be sure to prevent club root and cabbage root maggot.

Harvesting Allow the kales to grow and build up a good plant, then keep cutting at them. Early in the new year the heads of the kales may be removed, and then dozens of side growths will break out. These are first-class for food.

Varieties Hardy Sprouting; will withstand the most

rigorous winter. Extra Curled Scotch; a robust and compact variety, the leaves are densely curled. Asparagus Kale; a hardy late variety which can be sown where the crop is intended to be grown. Thousand-headed; very hardy, strong and branching, very productive and excellent for use in the spring.

SAVOYS

These can be regarded as a winter cabbage and, like the kales, are improved by frost. They are well worth growing because of their hardiness.

Soil and manuring Likes to be grown on firm ground, and is excellent to follow a crop like early potatoes or peas.

The soil should be prepared as advised for sprouts. In addition, wood ashes may be added at 2 ozs to the square yard and bone meal at 3 ozs per square yard.

Seed-sowing The seed should be sown in three batches; the first during the middle of March, the second at the beginning of April, and the third at the end of April.

The drills should be 9 ins apart, and directly the seedlings appear they should be thinned out to 3 ins apart. These thinnings may be transplanted to further beds, 6 ins square, if desired.

Planting The plants may be put out into their permanent position at the end of June and during the month of July. In the case of the smaller varieties the rows should be 18 ins apart and the plants 15 ins in the rows. With a stronger variety 2 ft square is advised.

Harvesting Cut directly the hearts are of a good size, and remove the stalk from the ground directly the savoy has been cut, as advised for cabbages.

Varieties Savoy King; light green, early, with round very solid hearts of excellent quality and flavour. Ice

Queen; hearts are solid uniform and of excellent quality. Ormskirk Late; exceedingly hardy, large headed and stands well. Winter King; large, short-stemmed and of first rate quality.

Cabbages – Drumhead type

5 Producing root crops

The root crops are important because they will keep. They provide very excellent food, not only during the late summer and autumn months, but also in the winter. Most of them are rich in vitamins A, B1, B2 and C.

The parsnip is particularly useful, because it can be left in the ground until required, and so takes up no storage room at all. Moreover, parsnips give 372 heat calories per pound – nearly three times as much as swedes, for instance.

BEETROOT

Beetroot may be grown quickly to be used during the summer, or sown to be harvested in the autumn and stored. They are not only excellent when used cold as a salad, but are first-class when boiled or steamed and served hot. They make excellent fritters.

Soil and manuring Beetroot grow best, perhaps, on a lightish soil, though they can be grown in almost all gardens.

Organic manure should not be dug in, for this tends to cause the beetroot to fork.

Seaweed has proved an excellent manure for beetroot, and may be applied at the rate of a barrow-load to 10 square yards. In addition long beetroot do very well on land that has carried celery or leeks the previous year.

Seed-sowing The seed should be sown at the end of April or the beginning of May. The rows should be 15 ins apart and the drills 2 ins deep. In the north, delay until May 15 if necessary.

Very early crops may be obtained on a sunny south border by sowing at the end of March, in rows 1 ft apart. Protection should be given to the young seedlings with black cotton or fish-netting against birds. The drills in this case are only $1\frac{1}{2}$ ins deep.

Another sowing of an early variety may be made in July, so as to obtain fresh young roots in the autumn and winter. Further details of such sowings are given in Chapter 9.

Thinning and transplanting Thinning should be done when the plants are 3 ins high, first of all to 4 ins apart, and then, when the roots are the size of golf balls, to 8 ins apart. These 'golf-ball' thinnings may be eaten.

Young beetroot thinnings may be transplanted if gaps should occur, but a good watering must be given every day afterwards until the plants are well established.

General cultivation The rows should be hoed if weeds appear, but the roots should never be damaged, for if they bleed, the colour is lost.

Harvesting Beetroot may be left in the ground until they are needed in the winter, providing the rows are covered with straw, bracken, etc., to guard against severe frost. Usually they are lifted and stored in a clamp, as advised for potatoes. The tops should be cut off before storing, but this should never be done too near to the crown, or bleeding may take place. It is possible to store in sand or in dry earth in a shed, and the roots will keep until the following June.

Varieties *Round-shaped:* Detroit New Globe; fine grained texture and probably the finest globe beet in existence. Burpees Golden; skin golden orange with bright yellow flesh – easy to grow and does not bleed. Foliage can be used as spinach.

Long-shaped: Formanova; fine grained in texture with excellent table qualities.

CARROTS

By various sowings of early maturing varieties and by

the judicious storing of main crops it is possible to have carrots all the year round. They contain 9 per cent of carbohydrates, and their calorific value stands at 193.

The shorthorns and forcing types should be grown in warm borders and in frames; the intermediates are often used as a main crop, especially on heavier soil, while the long types give the heaviest weight and do extraordinarily well on deep, sandy soil.

Soils and manuring Carrots prefer a deep, well-cultivated, sandy loam, but heavy soil should be improved by the addition of sandy or gritty material. On clays the shorter-rooted types should be grown.

Before sowing the seeds, the soil should be raked down into a fine condition. Then apply a good fish manure or seaweed manure at 4 ozs to the square yard. This is lightly raked in before seed sowing.

Seed-sowing A very early sowing may be made on a sunny south border or other warm spot in March, in drills 6 to 9 ins apart. Protection may be given to the rows by means of cloches, sacking or a frame-light or two.

The normal sowing will be in April, in drills $\frac{3}{4}$-inch deep and 12 to 18 ins apart, according to the variety. To ensure thin sowing, mix a little dry earth with the seed beforehand. Another sowing may be made in July. In this case the seed is sometimes broadcast instead of being sown in rows.

Thinning and transplanting If the early sowings have been done properly, there should be no need for thinning. The roots should be pulled early, while they are young. The same advice holds good for the July sowing. The main-crop sowings should be thinned to 6 or 9 ins apart, depending on the variety. The first thinning should be done to half the distance apart, and the second thinning to the final distance as advised for beetroot.

It is at this time that the greatest care should be taken

to keep away the carrot fly. Sowing alternate rows of carrots and onions keeps away the pests. Whizzed naphthalene should be applied along the rows for a few days before thinning and afterwards or powdered garlic can be used instead.

General cultivation To ensure quick germination it is advisable to give the rows a flooding from time to time. After this all that needs to be done is to hoe regularly.

Harvesting Before the winter frosts the roots should be lifted and stored in sand or dry earth in a shed. The tops should be cut off first of all. The roots may be put into a clamp, as described for potatoes.

Varieties Amsterdam Forcing Sweetheart; very early of deep colour and excellent flavour. Nantes Express; first class for forcing, long stump-rooted type with very little core. James' Scarlet Intermediate; a really good main crop of excellent flavour. St. Valery; main crop, superb quality, which keeps well.

PARSNIPS

This is one of the easiest vegetables to grow, and should be cultivated on a much larger scale. It is rich in food-value, it keeps well in the ground, and its only disadvantage is that it likes a long season of growth.

It is delicious steamed or boiled, served with white sauce. It is first-class par-boiled and baked in beef dripping, and it is excellent fried.

Soil and manuring Parsnips will grow in almost any soil. Those who have difficulty in getting long, straight roots, owing to stony ground, should bore holes with an iron rod, 3 ft deep and 3 ins in diameter at the top and 1 ft apart, and fill these up with sifted soil. Three seeds can then be sown on the top of each, the seedlings being thinned out to one if all grow.

As the seed is sown early, it is a good plan to dig the soil deeply in the autumn, and leave it rough. It is thus easier to fork down in February or March.

This crop should be grown on land that has been manured well the previous season, artificials being added as advised for main crop carrots. Meat and bone meal or a good fish manure may be applied as a top dressing a few days before seed-sowing, at 5 or 6 ozs per yard run.

Seed-sowing In the south the seed should be sown at the beginning of March, and in the north towards the end of March, providing the land is not too wet.

As the seed does not germinate well, it may be sown rather more thickly than carrots. The rows should be 18 ins apart and 1½ ins deep.

Thinning When the seedlings are an inch or so high, they should be thinned to 8 ins apart. If holes are bored, these are usually done a foot apart, because the roots grow very large in consequence.

General cultivation Regular hoeing.

Harvesting As has already been said, the roots may be left in the ground until required. If there is any danger of the ground being frozen so as to prevent the roots being dug up, a certain number of them may be lifted and stored in a clamp. Under ordinary conditions a little litter placed over the rows will prevent them being frozen.

Varieties *For shallow soils:* Offenham; intermediate size but with broad shoulders and excellent quality.

For deeper soils: Avon Resister; resistant to parsnip canker. Improved Hollow Crown; very large with a clear skin. Exhibition Long-rooted; fine flavour.

SWEDES

Garden swedes are valuable because they are so hardy in the winter. They are more delicate in flavour than the turnip, and have a calorific value of 145. They contain seven per cent of carbohydrates and two per cent of fibre.

The garden varieties of swedes are superior in food value to the farm types.

Soil and manuring Will grow on almost any soil. The light land should be enriched with compost and meat and bone meal, hoof and horn meal or a good fish manure may be applied at 4 ozs to the square yard. These should be raked in a few days before seed-sowing.

As seedlings are susceptible to club root, the surface of the soil should be limed with garden lime at the rate of 4 to 7 ozs per square yard, depending on the acidity of the soil.

Seed-sowing The seed should be sown in drills 18 ins apart. In the south the seed is usually sown in May and in the north early in June.

Thinning Thin out to 1 ft apart when the plants are 2 or 3 ins high.

General cultivation In very dry seasons flood the rows from time to time. Hoe regularly and dust, if necessary, with derris dust every two or three days to keep down the turnip flea-beetle. This is usually at its worst when the plants first come through.

Harvesting Like parsnips, the swedes may be left outside throughout the winter and dug up as desired. They are, for this reason, valuable, for they take up no storage room.

Varieties Purple-top Swede; clean, well-shaped roots of good colour. Bronze-top Swede; said by epicures to have the better flavour.

TURNIPS

Turnips may be grown as a main crop, to be used in the

winter, or there are the tennis-ball sized types of turnips which should be cooked when young.

It is possible to keep up a supply almost all the year round. Turnips are not as valuable as swedes, for their calorific value only stands at 95, and their carbohydrate value at 4, as against 7 in the case of swedes. Many people, however, do not care for the flavour of the swede.

Soil and manuring Turnips will do well on almost any soil except a shallow one. On a dry, droughty soil the roots have a tendency to run to seed, and are usually badly attacked by the flea-beetle.

It is not advisable to dig in large quantities of compost, but the top 3 ins should be enriched with sedge peat or powdered compost at ½ lb to the square yard, and, in addition, a good fish manure, meat and bone meal, or hoof and horn meal may be given at 4 or 5 ozs to the square yard.

Seed-sowing There are four periods when the seed may be sown:

1 *In the frame*. Sow the seed in holes made 1 inch deep and 4 ins apart each way. Drop four seeds in a hole and thin out to one if all grow. After sowing, fill in the holes. The frame should be heated or over a hot-bed. Turnips will not stand a great deal of forcing, and the frames should be given as much ventilation as possible from the time the seedlings are through.

2 *Outside, early*. A sowing may be made in the early part of March if the ground can be got down to a fine tilth. The rows should be 4 ins apart and 1 inch deep. The seedlings should be thinned out to 4 ins apart.

Another sowing may be made in April, the drills being 12 ins apart, the plants being thinned to 6 ins apart when they are 1 inch high.

3 *The main sowing*. The main sowing is usually done in May – if possible in a shady situation. The rows should be 1 ft apart, the turnips thinned out to 6 ins apart.

The roots from such a sowing are pulled in the late summer.

4 *Winter turnips.* Seed should be sown any time from the middle of July till the end of August, the drills being 18 ins apart, and the plants thinned to 6 ins apart when 2 ins high. When fit to use, a further thinning should be done to a foot apart.

General cultivation A sharp look-out must be kept for the turnip flea-beetle, especially in the early stages, and regular dustings with derris dust should be given.

In dry seasons it may be necessary to give a good flooding once a week or so. Regular hoeings are also necessary.

Harvesting Pull the spring and summer sown varieties while they are young and fresh, and before they get coarse.

The main crop turnips may be dug up in the autumn, before the sharp frosts occur, and should be stored as advised for carrots and potatoes.

Winter turnips may be left outside until desired for use.

Varieties Purple Top Milan; earlier than any other. Tokyo Cross; perfect globe-shaped roots, pure white and excellent quality. Snowball Early White Stone; first class for general use. Golden Ball; best variety for autumn sowing, hardy and remains in good condition for a very long time.

TURNIP TOPS

The green leaves of the turnip tops are useful and tasty as a vegetable, and are of great value when greens are scarce.

Another great advantage is that this vegetable may be sown as late as the first weeks in September for use in late February, March and early April.

The rows should be 2 ft apart, and the seed should be sown thinly. No thinning should be done, and the crop should be allowed to grow naturally.

The leaves should be pulled as required, and though good roots are not to be expected, it is sometimes possible to use some of the roots that develop when the leaf part of the crop has been harvested.

KOHL RABI

See Chapter 10.

SALSIFY

See Chapter 10.

6 Delicious peas and beans

This chapter deals with the ordinary peas and beans that one expects to find in the garden or allotment. The special beans that are often useful in an emergency, like Dutch beans and Soya beans, are dealt with in Chapter 10.

Runner beans are very useful, for they can be made to clamber up the iron railings at the end of a garden, or to cover a shed; they can be grown up wire-netting and growing up poles they form a good background to the herbaceous border. They are very heavy cropping, they last for a good time, and they contain vitamins A, B2 and C.

Broad beans are useful, especially those that are sown in the autumn and come into use in the spring. French beans have their place because they can be sown in May, as a summer crop, and again in June and July for the autumn.

Peas, too, are eighteen per cent carbohydrate, and from that point of view are as good as parsnips, old potatoes and salsify, and considerably better than most other vegetables. Their calorific content is higher than that of new potatoes, and almost five times as high as cauliflower or artichokes. Another advantage is that they can be sown in the autumn and then from spring until midsummer. The dwarf varieties will be perhaps the most useful in times of emergency, for they do not need sticks.

Another important point in favour of peas and beans is that they add nitrogen to the ground if their roots are left in after harvesting. They thus enrich the soil, and leave it in a better condition than when the seed was sown.

BROAD BEANS

The 'straw' of the broad bean is quite useful when dried

and may be used to form mats to give protection to plants in frames, or if erected between poles, to act as windbreaks.

Soil and manuring The broad bean will grow on almost any soil, and no special preparation is needed other than plain forking. Good compost may be applied at the rate of one good barrow-load per 10 square yards, in addition to which meat and bone meal or a good fish manure should be applied at the same time at 4 ozs to the square yard.

Seed-sowing A sowing of the long-pod types may be made in November and January, while the Broad Windsor group should be sown during March or April. November sowings are not always successful, owing to frost or wet weather.

The rows should be 2 ft 6 ins apart. The drills should be drawn out 5 ins wide. A double row of beans should be placed in these drills, zigzag fashion, so that they are 6 ins apart. The drills should be 4 ins deep.

If dwarf varieties are grown double rows should be arranged, 9 ins apart, with the seeds placed 6 ins apart in each row. The double rows should be 2 ft apart from one another.

Twelve beans should be sown in a group at the ends of each row, or at the ends of each double row, and the plants that result may be used for filling up any gaps that appear a few weeks later.

General cultivation Hoe if necessary. Keep a sharp look-out for the black aphis. Directly this appears, dust or spray with derris. It is not necessary to pinch out the tops, except to encourage the early production of beans.

Directly the crop is over the plants should be cut down and the roots left in the ground. The tops may be rotted down for manure, or as stated in the introduction, may be dried and made into temporary mats.

Harvesting Pick the beans regularly when young, as this ensures a heavier crop.

Varieties Major; earliest maturing, with high yield and good quality. Long-fellow; produces pods of exceptional length, quality and flavour with quite ordinary culture. The Sutton; sturdy bush like plants, heavy croppers.

Pinching out the tops of broad beans helps prevent blackfly and encourages growth

FRENCH BEANS
(Sometimes called the Dwarf or Kidney bean.)

It is useful because it comes into cropping earlier than its cousin, the runner bean. Withstands drought better than any other vegetable crop.

Soil and manuring On the whole, the French bean prefers a light soil to a heavy one. The land should be prepared as advised for broad beans, only the ground where the French beans are to be grown may be cropped with lettuce first of all, and these give some protection for the young plants as they come through. Further, the plants are friends. This is an excellent method of inter-cropping (taking two crops from one piece of land).

Lime is necessary for all members of the pea and bean family and may be applied to the surface of the ground at from 4 to 7 ozs per square yard, depending on the acidity of the soil. The soil can always be tested, of course, with a B.D.H. Soil Indicator. (Fellows of *The Good Gardeners' Association* can get their soil tested free.)

Seed-sowing It is possible to make a sowing in frames in March, and when the plants are through they can be transplanted to other frames, 8 ins square, or they may be thinned, and grown on in the same frame.

Another sowing may be made early in April in a frame, but the plants that result are put outside in a sheltered border in the second or third week of May. When trans-planting French beans, plenty of soil should be kept around the roots.

The first sowing outside should be done during the first week of May, or even earlier in the south-west. Drills should be made 2 ins deep and 4 ins wide, and from 2 to 3 ft apart, depending on the height of the variety. In each drill the beans should be planted zigzag fashion, 6 ins apart.

It is quite possible to sow twice as thickly as this, and to thin out after three weeks', transplanting the seedlings into gaps or into further rows.

The last sowing of the season should be done during the first week of July. The rows should be 2 ft apart, and the beans spaced out 10 ins apart. This spacing is usually done by thinning plants which are sown two or three times thicker than this.

General cultivation Regular hoeing is necessary, and the soil should be drawn up to the plants rather than away from them. On rich soil the taller plants may need supporting with bushy twigs if the situation is rather exposed.

Harvesting The beans should be picked when young. Regular gatherings will cause an increase in the crop.

Varieties Masterpiece; useful for forcing or outdoor work, a heavy cropper with long handsome pods. Processor; stringless and of high quality and highly resistant to adverse weather. Flair; extra early or useful for autumn use from late sowings, heavy cropper with stringless pods.

RUNNER BEANS

As the introduction suggests, they can be grown almost anywhere where they can have an extensive root run.

Soil and manuring It is an advantage to have deep soil, and the ground where the beans are to be grown should be liberally composted.

Compost should be applied at the rate of one barrow-load to 10 square yards. Garden lime should be applied to the surface of the ground afterwards at, say, 3 ozs per square yard.

Apply also a good fish manure or seaweed manure at 3 ozs to the square yard and lightly rake in before the seed is sown.

Seed-sowing It is not generally possible to sow runner beans until early in May, and in the north until the second or third week in May. For succession another sowing may be made early in June.

When the beans are to grow up poles, wire-netting, or string, the rows should be 5 ft apart; but where they are to be kept cut back, and are grown on the flat, the rows may be 3½ ft apart.

The seed is usually planted 2 ins deep and 6 ins apart in the rows. Sometimes a wide drill is drawn out, and the beans are then put in zigzag fashion in the drill, 8 ins apart.

A number of beans are sown in a group at the end of the row, so that the seedlings may be transplanted into any blank spaces that appear when they are 3 ins or so high.

Staking The poles are usually put into position just after sowing, and may be 1 ft apart. Double rows of poles are sometimes used, and these are joined together at the top by means of a cross pole, forming a series of inverted V's.

In an emergency it would probably be impossible to obtain bean poles, and structures should therefore be erected consisting of wire-netting, string, and the like.

General cultivation Runner beans that are grown on the flat should be kept 'topped' from time to time, the tops of the plants being pinched out when they are 18 ins high. This causes them to break out into further growth. A further pinching back should take place when the subsequent growths are 18 ins long. After this the growth should be kept cut back with a pair of shears from time to time.

There is a variety, Hammond, which is dwarf like the French bean. The seed of this variety may be sown in rows 3 ft apart and the plants do not have to be cut back as in the case of the climbing types.

Hoeing should be carried out if necessary, the soil being drawn up to the plants rather than away from them.

Late in June a mulch of sedge peat or powdered compost should be put along the rows to keep in the moisture. This should be done after a heavy watering and is particularly valuable in a dry season.

In the evening the rows may be sprayed with tepid water, as this helps the flowers to set and keeps the pods tender.

Harvesting Picking should be done regularly. Pods that have to be picked to prevent them from seeding may be kept fresh for several days, if they are stood upright in water, on their stem ends. At the end of the season the plants may be cut down to within an inch of soil level, and, being perennials, they will grow again the following spring.

Varieties Hammonds White; has an excellent flavour and needs no staking, for early cropping it is ideal under cloches. Kelvedon Marvel; exceedingly prolific and good quality. Crusader; one of the longest podded varieties, produces large clusters of broad, massive, fleshy pods of fine quality and texture.

HARICOT BEANS

The haricot bean or haricot vert is not grown enough in this country. The idea is to grow a bean similar to the French bean, but the seeds are allowed to develop, and these are removed from the pods as in the case of broad beans or peas, and are then cooked.

They should be treated in a similar manner to French beans throughout their growth. The best variety is Green Gem.

WAX-POD BEAN

This is sometimes called the butter bean (but must not be confused with the large white bean sold in grocers' shops, dried, as the butter bean). It grows like the French bean, but bears yellow pods. The whole pod is used.

The best variety is Golden Wax Pod.

Giant Wax Pod is a golden runner bean.

PEAS

Peas, like beans, have nodules on their roots containing

bacteria which extract nitrogen from the air. The roots should therefore be left in the ground after harvesting.

Soil and manuring Peas will grow on almost any soil, providing they are well limed so as to counteract acidity.

They are on the ground for only a short time, and so the plant foods that are used should be in an available form, or should be put on some time beforehand, so that they are in such a form that the roots can use them when they want them.

Good compost should be applied at one large barrow-load to 10 square yards. In addition, 3 ozs of fish manure or seaweed manure should be used per square yard.

Directly the plants are through, dried blood may be applied at 2 ozs per yard run, in order to give the plants a start. The organic content of the soil may be increased at any time by the addition of meat and bone meal at 4 ozs per square yard.

Seed-sowing It is convenient to sow the seed in flat drills which have been drawn out beforehand, 5 to 6 ins wide and 3 ins deep. In these drills the seed should be sown 2 ins apart each way, and for the later varieties, 3 ins apart. It is never advisable to sow peas thicker than this.

To prevent birds or mice getting the seeds, they should be soaked in a mixture of paraffin and red lead, made into the consistency of ordinary cream.

When the plants are coming through, the rows should be protected with home-made or bought pea guards.

Except in the north the first sowing should be made in the autumn, in November and December. For such sowings it is a good plan to draw the drill out in the morning on a warm day, so as to let it dry out before actually sowing the seed in the afternoon.

A further early sowing may be made at the beginning of February or in the north at the beginning of March. Dwarf varieties should be chosen (round seeded ones) the rows being 18 ins apart.

Similar varieties may be sown in pots or boxes, in frames or the greenhouse, late in January or early in February. The plants thus raised should be put out in the border late in March or early in April.

From the beginning of April onwards peas may be sown at regular intervals. Quite a good plan (if there is enough room) is to make another sowing directly the last row is seen above ground.

The earliest maturing varieties may be sown again late in June or the beginning of July, so as to get good pickings in the month of September. Such sowings may follow potatoes or early cauliflowers.

The soil should be given a good flooding, if possible, and this will not only hasten the germination of the seeds, but will also give the young plants a good start.

The distance between one row and another depends on the variety sown. A 3 ft variety needs an 18 inch space between the rows, while a 4 ft variety should have a 2 ft space.

General cultivation Hoeing should be done if necessary. Mulches may be given along the rows as advised for runner beans. If the weather is dry, a good watering may be given from time to time in small trenches drawn out on either side of the row, rather than in the row itself.

To help the plants to climb, bushy twigs should be inserted in the ground near the peas when they are 3 or 4 inches high. Whenever peasticks cannot be bought, wire-netting or nylon netting may be used instead. This should be kept upright with bamboos inserted into the soil to give support. Dwarf varieties will, however, grow quite well without support.

Harvesting Peas should be picked regularly and no pods should be missed when ready.

Varieties *Early:* Histon Mini; about 12 ins, pods well filled with peas of excellent flavour. Meteor; 1½ ft, heavy cropper, can be sown in autumn or spring. Kelvedon Wonder; 1½ ft, prolific cropper, well filled pods.

Main crop: Hurst Green Shaft; 2½ ft, disease resistant and excellent flavour. Onward; 2 ft, immense cropper, well filled pods hanging in pairs.

7 Potatoes are necessary

The potato is certainly an important crop, but it is more cheaply grown on a large scale with tractors and ploughs than it is in the private garden. Transport is, however, always an important factor in times of economic stress, and so it may be important to grow large quantities of potatoes in and near all towns and villages.

Not only are more potatoes eaten than any other vegetable, but they are an excellent cleaning crop. New potatoes are more valuable than old potatoes (they are free of disease and last longer), and are also richer in vitamins. It is therefore suggested that the householder should concentrate on earliest and mid-season varieties if he has a limited-sized garden or allotment.

Soil Potatoes can be grown on all soils, though some produce those of an inferior flavour to others. It is said that the heavy clays and peaty soils produce waxy tubers. Damp, badly drained, or low-lying land should be avoided, although even such a situation may be productive of good and sound crops if the summer is hot and dry. Situations which are confined or over-hung by large trees are also unsuitable.

The best potatoes are grown in an open, sunny situation in deep, well-drained, medium soil – not a pure clay or too light a sand. A clay can be made friable, but it is difficult to work during wet periods, which is a nuisance during harvesting and planting times.

Preparation of the soil One of the best ways of preparing the soil for potatoes is by working into the strip where the potato sets are to be planted, plenty of powdery good compost. I use a bucketful to the yard run at least. The rows should run north and south, so that the winter sun can fall equally on either side of the rows. The rain will also penetrate the soil and 'sweeten' it.

The soil may be ridged up slightly in the spring, a week or so before planting, the organic fertilizers being put into the bottom of the ridges.

Manuring The land should be given its layer of compost in the autumn, but more can be put in the rows at planting time. In addition fish manure or seaweed manure should be applied in the rows at 3 ozs per yard row.

It is most important to buy seed either of Scottish or Irish origin. Tubers should be got from plants free from virus diseases. With any seed purchased the grower should obtain the certificate number. This is his guarantee.

The tubers used for seed should be about the size of a hen's egg, and should weigh about 2 ozs. Those who obtain larger tubers should cut these in such a way that each half contains the necessary 'eyes'. This cutting should take place just before the tubers are planted. If done earlier, loss of crop results.

If the potatoes are bought early in the year (and this is a good plan) they should be 'boxed up' – that is to say, placed in shallow trays to sprout, rose end upwards. (The rose end is the end where most of the eyes are found, and is the opposite end to that which was attached to the underground stem.) This ensures an earlier and heavier yield.

You can use what is called a potato tray, 2 ft 6 ins long, 1 ft 6 ins wide, and 3½ ins deep. In the corners there are small square posts standing 3 ins above the sides. These posts are there so that the trays may be stood one above the other while the sprouting process is going on, without injuring the sprout.

These trays containing the potatoes should then be stacked in any cool, light airy place where there is no possibility of their being frozen. Some gardeners use a cool greenhouse, while others find a loft or a shed quite convenient. Air should circulate freely amongst the trays, and the potatoes should be looked over occasionally to remove any that are going rotten.

When the tubers start to sprout they should be disbudded, leaving only the two strongest shoots at the rose end of the tubers. When the time comes for planting, the trays should be carried out into the garden. The tubers should then be taken out one at a time and placed carefully in the bottom of a shallow furrow without breaking off the sprouts. If planting is done carelessly, the sprouts will break off easily, and all the trouble spent on them in the trays will be wasted.

The object of sprouting the seed is to secure a few weeks' growth before planting takes place. Sprouted potatoes are, therefore, ready to harvest several weeks earlier than potatoes planted unsprouted. This saving of time also ensures heavier crops, as the potatoes have, in consequence, a longer season of growth.

Planting The earliest potatoes should be planted in ridges 18 ins apart, the tubers being planted 12 ins apart in the rows. For this earliest planting the tubers should be harvested when they are quite small.

The rows for ordinary early potatoes should be 1 ft 9 ins apart, the seed being placed 12 ins apart in the rows. The rows for second earlies should be 2 ft 3 ins apart, the seed being 1 ft 3 ins apart in the rows. For the main crop the rows should be 2 ft 6 ins apart and the tubers 1 ft 6 ins apart in the rows.

No seed potatoes should be planted deeper than 2–3 ins and with the earliest varieties 1 or 2 ins will do. The rows should run north and south, and, after planting, the soil and compost should be drawn over the rows, so as to leave a slight ridge and mark where they are.

Planting should take place in the south in about the third week of March, and in the north as late as the second week of April. Though it sounds peculiar to say so, it is better to plant the late potatoes first, and the early potatoes last. The lates have a longer season of growth and are not through the ground soon enough to be affected by a late spring frost.

General cultivation Directly the foliage appears through the ground the rows should be lightly hoed with a draw hoe; three weeks later more compost may be applied all along the rows in order to keep the growing tubers in the dark. If there is any fear of frost, the soil may be drawn up over the plant, and then, when the frost is over, this soil should be drawn back again. Another method is to cover the potato tops with sheets of newspaper when the BBC gives a frost warning.

When the tops are half-grown they should be earthed up say 6 ins deep. At this time the stems of the plant will be about 8 ins high.

The next earthing-up should be done three weeks after the first, another inch of soil being brought up to the stems. Further earthings-up may be done if necessary. The ridges should never be earthed up too steeply, as, if this is done, the tubers may go green at the sides.

A sharp look out should be kept for the potato blight from June onwards, and directly there is any sign of the disease, the leaves and stems should be given a thorough spraying with Bordeaux Mixture.

The flat system Planting on the flat can be done on light composted land. Rake it into a good tilth in the normal way. At planting time shallow holes like nests are prepared along a line marked out, one for each potato. The soil and compost from the second row of holes is used to cover up those in the first row, and so on to the end of the plot.

The lazy-bed system This system is useful on soil where the water-level is near the surface. It consists of making raised beds 4 or 5 ft wide, with deep trenches between the beds which drain away the superfluous moisture. The seed tubers are placed on the surface, one row at each side of the bed. Soil is taken from between the beds to cover the seed and again to earth up the plants, and in this way the trenches are formed.

How to raise potatoes mid-June Good seed should be purchased, and this should be sprouted, as previously advised. A piece of ground should be selected in a sheltered position and which is inclined to the south or south-west. This should be forked lightly and really good compost added liberally. A further quantity of compost should then be prepared consisting half of good compost and the other half of equal quantities of wood ashes and medium grade sedge peat and sand, together with a little old soot.

In mid-February the ground should be ridged up into ridges, 8 ins high and 20 ins apart. In March 2 ins of compost should be laid in the bottom of each ridge. The sprouted sets should be laid on this, 10 ins apart, and be covered with 2 ins more of the compost. As the tops begin to show, a little fine earth may be drawn over them, and if it threatens to be frosty at night time, give protection by the use of sacking erected over some temporary framework.

With this system a good crop should be harvested at the end of the second week of June.

Lifting and storing The rows of early potatoes may be lifted as soon as the tubers are of a suitable size. The lifting should be done on a fine day if possible, and the potatoes will come out clean and bright, and look far more attractive.

The main crop need not be lifted to be stored until the haulm has died down. If, however, the haulm is diseased, it should be cut off and burned, as if it is allowed to die down naturally, it may cause the crop to rot.

The early and second early potatoes will be dug up and used as desired. The main crops will be harvested and be stored in clamps (or hogs, pies or hales, as they are called in various districts). When the tubers are coated with soil, this should be rubbed off with the hands before clamping.

The ground on which the clamp is to stand should, if possible, be higher than the general level. In no case should it be lower.

Before clamping, the potatoes should be fairly dry, and any showing traces of disease should be removed and used immediately.

The tubers should be piled up in a long, ridge-shaped heap about 3½ ft high and 3 ft wide. They should then be covered with straw or bracken or other dry litter to a depth of about 6 ins and over the straw a 6-inch covering of soil should be placed neatly.

The surface should be made smooth and firm with the spade so that the rain will run off. The soil for covering should be taken from the ground outside the clamp, and during this operation a trench is cut all round to carry away the water, and so keep the contents dry. Ventilating holes should be cut through the top of the ridge about 6 ft apart and a tuft of straw pulled through each hole and allowed to project. These tufts should be twisted.

If there is enough room in good dry buildings, potatoes may be stored here instead of being clamped. A good thickness of straw should be put between the potatoes and the outside walls, and they should be well covered on top to protect them from frost and to exclude light.

Varieties *Earlies:* Suttons Foremost; a very heavy cropping white skinned oval variety, cooks very well; it produced 4 lbs large tubers per plant at Arkley Manor in 1975. Arran Pilot; an early kidney-shaped variety. Ulster Chieftain; a very kind, a floury cooker.

Main crops: Pentland Grown; heavy cropper, shallow eyes, white flash, good quality. Maris Peer; an early type of main crop, heavy cropper, delicious to eat.

Special note. These are all 'immune' varieties. This means they are immune to wart disease though not to all other diseases. Under the Ministry of Agriculture's regulations those who have land subject to this disease must grow immune varieties only.

8 Other valuable vegetables

A glance through any seedman's catalogue or the study of some complete book on vegetables will reveal that there are a very large number of vegetables that can be grown in this country. It is the aim of this book, however, to concentrate on those crops that are of the greatest value from the feeding point of view and those that can be grown in any beginner's garden. Chapters 4, 5, 6 and 7 deal with the main vegetables; Chapter 9 with salads and herbs, and Chapter 10 with one or two unusual vegetables that are worthwhile including.

This chapter has been reserved for the vegetables that for one reason or another do not fit into the other chapters.

White trench-grown celery has not been included, for it takes up a good deal of room, it is a long time in coming to maturity, and needs special cultivation and blanching. In an emergency the self-bleaching celery might well be grown in its place.

ARTICHOKE, JERUSALEM

This is a vegetable that ought to be far more popular than it is. It is very easy to grow and contains seven per cent of carbohydrates.

Soil and manuring It will grow in almost any soil and will produce heavy crops under indifferent treatment. The heaviest yields result when the land is given compost at one large barrow-load to 12 square yards. In addition a good seaweed manure like Marinure can be given at 3 ozs to the yard run.

Planting The artichoke may be grown at the bottom of the garden, and forms an excellent screen. It can be grown equally well alongside fences or, of course, in rows. These, because of the height of the stems, should be 2 ft 6 ins apart. The tubers, which should be about the size of a pullet's egg, are planted, 12 ins apart and 6 ins deep.

Planting is done as for potatoes.

General cultivation Directly the plants are through, the ground should be hoed, and when the growths are well above the soil, the rows may be earthed up somewhat. Towards the end of November the stems should be cut down to within a foot of the ground.

Harvesting It is possible to lift the whole crop at one time and to store the tubers in sand, but better to lift the roots as required in the winter, the egg-sized tubers being selected for planting the following season.

Varieties Fuseau has a much better flavour than the old-fashioned knobbly types. Fuseau has smooth skin free from lumpiness. (*The Good Gardeners' Association* has it.)

CELERY – SELF-BLEACHING OR BLANCHING

Soil and manuring The soil should be bastard trenched and enriched with plenty of farmyard manure or other organic matter. In addition, a good fish manure or hoof and horn meal should be used at 5 or 6 ozs per square yard.

Seed-sowing The seed may be sown in boxes, filled with Alex No-soil compost, and placed on the staging of the greenhouse at a temperature of 60–65°F. A fortnight later the seedlings should be pricked out into further boxes, 3 ins apart. Those who have not got a greenhouse may sow the seed on soil over a hot-bed in a frame, ½ oz of seed being sufficient for a frame 6 ft long by 4 ft wide.

It is as well to obtain seed that has been treated with formaldehyde, as a guarantee that it is not infected with celery rust.

Those who have no facilities for seed-sowing should obtain plants from a nurseryman, or should make arrangements with a seedsman to supply plants at the right time.

The plants should be put out in rows 18 ins apart and 1 ft apart in the rows. Dwarf varieties need be only 1 ft square. The ground should be well soaked afterwards. The following day the bed should be given a hoeing, so as to leave the surface rough.

General cultivation Though the celery is self-bleaching, and can, therefore, be grown 'on the flat', it is better to place straw among the plants in the autumn so as to ensure that the stems are really white. Some people prefer to tie a stiff paper collar around each plant.

Harvesting Dig up and use when sufficiently blanched.

Varieties Lathom Self Blanching; compact, solid yellow sticks, crisp, nutty and free from string. Golden Self Blanching; compact, dwarf, solid yellow heads of good flavour and free from strings.

LEEKS

A very valuable vegetable indeed is the leek, for it can be used in the winter time when other vegetables are scarce. Leeks may be dug up as required, and do not have to be lifted and stored. The severest of winters cannot harm the plants.

Soil and manuring The leek can be grown on practically any soil providing it has been properly composted. It prefers a soil in which there is plenty of organic matter present and one which contains moisture without being sodden.

Leeks may be grown on the flat rather than in trenches.

In addition to the compost that is raked in, dried poultry manure may be used at 2 ozs to the square yard, wood ashes at 4 ozs to the square yard, and bone meal at 3 ozs to the square yard.

Halfway through the growing season, seaweed manure

should be applied at 3 ozs to the yard run.

Seed-sowing The seed may be sown in gentle heat under glass towards the end of January. The Alex No-soil compost is used and placed in boxes, and the seed sown thinly on this. The boxes are then stood on the benches of a greenhouse at a temperature of about 60°F. The usual care should be taken about watering and covering the boxes with a sheet of glass and a piece of brown paper until the seedlings have germinated.

When the plants are an inch or so high they should be pricked out into other boxes, in somewhat richer soil, 1½ ins apart. The boxes should then be watered and placed on the shelf in the greenhouse, near the light, and kept at a temperature of about 55°F. When the plants are 5 or 6 ins high they should be gradually hardened off.

Those who have no greenhouse can sow the seed in the open, or in frames, about the middle of March. In the open the drills should be 18 ins apart, and in the frame 9 ins apart. As soon as the seedlings can be handled they should be transplanted into another border or into a frame, 8 ins square. Here they may grow on until they are 6 or 9 ins high, when they can be planted out.

Planting The plants should be taken out of the soil carefully, so as not to break the roots. If the roots are damaged, the leaves should be cut back, so as to balance things up.

'On the flat' the rows should be 1 ft apart and the plants 8 ins apart in the rows. Holes should be made with a dibber 9 ins deep and the leeks should be dropped into the hole. A little water should be poured into the holes after planting, but the holes need not be filled in.

Another method of planting is to make drills 9 ins apart and 6 ins deep, and to plant the young leeks in these 8 ins apart.

General cultivation Hoe in between the rows if necessary.

Harvesting Dig up as required from December onwards.

Varieties Marble Pillar; given the same conditions, it produces solid white stems up to twenty-five per cent longer than any other variety. Musselburgh; one of the finest varieties, with long thick stems – also very hardy. Malines Winter; a very promising new leek which matures late and is of excellent quality.

ONIONS

The onion is one of the most popular vegetables: hundreds of tons are imported annually from abroad, but it is possible for the householder to grow sufficient for his own use. It is a vegetable that will keep quite easily. The English onion is much more valuable than the Spanish onion, and can, of course, be grown for salad purposes also.

Soil and manuring On the whole, onions do best on a deep sandy, rich loam. They will, however, do well on a heavy clay, providing this is opened up by the addition of finely divided organic matter like compost or sedge peat.

The soil should be prepared some time before seed sowing, so as to allow it to settle down. Compost should be added at the rate of one good barrow-load to 10 square yards. In addition, the following may be added: 4 ozs of fish manure or seaweed manure per square yard; wood ashes may be used as well at ½ lb per square yard and so may soot at ¼ lb to the square yard, and dried poultry manure at 3 ozs to the square yard if this is available.

It is advisable to firm the surface of the soil before sowing the seed, by treading. Firming should never be done when the soil is sticky however.

Seed-sowing in spring During the month of March in the south and April in the north, seed should be sown in rows 1 ft apart and ½-inch deep. To cover the drills it should only be necessary to give a very light raking.

General cultivation Hoeing should be done if necessary directly the crop is visible, the soil being drawn away from the rows, rather than up to them. Thinning should be done as soon as possible, so as to leave little groups 3 ins apart, and later these should be thinned to 6 ins apart. The onions thus pulled supply material for salad. Eventually these little groups are thinned down to one plant, which should produce a good bulb.

It is at thinning time that the onion fly has the opportunity of laying her eggs, and to prevent this, whizzed naphthalene should be applied along the rows. The onion fly can be kept at bay if carrots are grown between the rows – the idea being to have one row of onions, one row of carrots, another row of onions, and so on.

Harvesting The bulbs should ripen naturally in September but, to help them, the tops are usually bent over at the neck. After this the onions may be stored in a cool, airy, dry place. It is possible to hang them up in groups under the eaves of a building or in a potting or tool shed.

Seed-sowing in autumn Seed should be sown cither in the latter part of July or the beginning of August. The farther north, the earlier the sowing. For purely salad onions the rows should be 9 ins apart, but for onions that are to bulb early the rows should be 1 ft apart.

Such crops usually follow the harvesting of a well-manured crop, such as early peas, early potatoes, early carrots, etc., and so it is only necessary to rake the ground finely and draw out the drills.

General cultivation Hoeing should be carried out if necessary. For the salad onions no thinning is done. The plants should be pulled out as required. The varieties that are to bulb are thinned in the spring and the thinnings transplanted, 1 ft between the rows and 6 to 9 ins between the plants.

Harvesting They should be ready for use in August.

Seed-sowing – pickling Those who have an odd corner of poor soil and wish to grow onions with little or no soil preparation, should grow pickling onions.

The seed should be broadcast over the surface of the soil in April, and lightly raked in. The crop is kept weeded, but is not thinned.

Harvesting Pickling onions are ready in September as a rule.

Varieties *Spring sown:* Bedfordshire Champion; mild flavour, heavy cropper, firm and a good keeper. Ailsa Craig; rich golden straw colour, one of the best all purpose varieties.

Onions, showing how the tops are bent over to help ripening. Note how two rows bend towards each other.

Autumn sown salad: White Lisbon; the favourite silver-skinned variety for pulling green. The Queen; small silver-skinned variety for salads.

Autumn sown bulbing: Unwins Reliance; usually a long-keeping onion of good size, ripens in the summer.

Pickling: Silver Skin; of delicate flavour, early. The Queen; smaller but very quick growing.

SHALLOTS

As shallots are one of the easiest vegetables to grow and are not as a rule attacked by the onion fly, they will prove an excellent crop in a national emergency.

Soil and manuring Shallots will grow on almost any soil, providing it has been well worked and is well drained. Fish manure may be applied as advised for onions and, in addition, hoof and horn meal may be raked into the top 2 ins at the rate of 3 ozs to the square yard.

Planting In the south it should be possible to get the planting done early in February, and in the north during the second or third week of March. The rows should be 1 ft apart and the bulbs spaced out 4 ins apart in the rows.

Before planting, the soil should be firmed, and the bulbs then pushed in to half their depth. Any loose skins or dead tops should be removed. A fortnight after planting, the bed should be examined and the bulbs firmed. Any that have gone rotten should be replaced.

Planting can be done in any odd place – for instance, along the tops of celery trenches, as an edging to a path, or in between rows of fruit bushes.

General cultivation The rows should be hoed if necessary, but not deeply. Care should be taken not to bury the bulbs.

Harvesting In July the leaves of the shallot will be seen to be turning yellow, and by the second or third week the bulbs should be lifted and left on the surface of the soil to dry off. After a few days they may be placed on a path or a concrete yard in the sun. They should be turned over two or three times so as to make certain they are thoroughly dry. After this they should be divided and stored in a cool, dry place.

Varieties Russian, Dutch or Jersey Shallot; produces a larger and rounder bulb than the true variety. The skin is coppery-red and the leaves are greyish-green. Yields a heavy crop, but does not keep as well as the true shallot.

True Red or Yellow Shallot; produces a nice firm bulb of the right size for pickling. Keeps well.

SPINACH

A very valuable vegetable, spinach is rich in vitamins A, B1 and B2. Is moderately high in calorific value, and contains a percentage of iron, calcium and phosphorus.

There are various kinds: Summer, Winter, Spinach Beet, Seakale Spinach and New Zealand Spinach; these will all be dealt with under separate headings.

ANNUAL SPINACH – SUMMER AND WINTER

Soil and manuring The annual spinach will grow almost anywhere. It goes to seed quickly on very light soils, and to prevent this plenty of moisture-holding material should be incorporated.

When preparing the ground, home-made compost should be added at the rate of one good barrow-load to 12 square yards. In addition, meat and bone meal, hoof and horn meal or a good fish manure may be forked into the ground at the rate of 4 or 5 ozs to the square yard. Fish manure may be given in small dressings along the rows three times, at fortnightly intervals, directly the plants have started into growth.

Seed-sowing Summer spinach should be sown once a fortnight from the beginning of March onwards in order to keep up the supply. As the weather gets warmer the sowings should be made in the shadier situations of the garden. In a small garden quite short rows will do. The drills should be 1 ft apart and 1 inch deep, and directly the seedlings can be handled, they should be thinned out to 6 ins apart.

Winter spinach should be sown from the first week in August to the middle of September, once a fortnight. It is often necessary in the north and west to make special raised beds of 5 ft wide, 3 ins above the level of the soil around. This keeps the beds dry. Under this system the rows should be 9 ins apart and the seedlings are thinned to 4 ins apart.

General cultivation The winter spinach may need protection. This can be done by using straw over the rows and between them. Bracken or heather is useful too, and so of course, are continuous cloches or Access frames.

Harvesting Summer spinach should be picked regularly and quite hard. It does not matter if the majority of leaves are removed from a plant.

Winter spinach should not be picked hard. The largest leaves should be taken, and these should be gathered singly.

Varieties *Summer:* Monarch Long Standing; the best round-seeded variety. New Zealand; forms a low-growing rather creeping plant, producing thick, fleshy, arrow-shaped leaves.

Winter: Broad Leaved Prickly; a large leaved hardy strain, very long standing.

SPINACH BEET

This is a perpetual spinach, and produces a continuous supply of large leaves during spring, summer and autumn.

Soil and manuring See instructions for beetroot (Chapter 5).

Seed-sowing The seed should be sown in April, and another sowing in August. In this way it should be possible to pick spinach all the year. The rows should be 15 ins apart and the plants should be thinned out to 18 ins apart in the rows.

General cultivation Regular weeding, hoeing and occasional waterings are all that are necessary to keep the plants cropping satisfactorily.

Harvesting The leaves should be gathered regularly directly they are large enough. If this is not done, the older leaves will begin to get coarse. It is necessary to pick the leaves stem and all, so as to ensure further leaves developing.

SEAKALE SPINACH

The Seakale beet or Seakale spinach is grown for the thick white stems it produces and for the large green leaves growing at the ends of these stems. The latter are used as spinach, and the former as seakale.

Soil and manuring As for beetroot.

Seed-sowing Seeds should be sown thinly late in April or early in May, in drills 15 ins apart. Plants should be spaced out to 9 ins apart in the rows.

General cultivation Only regular weeding, hoeing and occasional watering necessary.

Harvesting The leaves and stems should be pulled regularly, and should not be cut. If the leaves are removed without the stems, cropping is impeded.

VEGETABLE MARROW

The marrow is a crop that is quite easy to grow in any odd corner. It is quite suitable for covering up a mound or for growing up a fence, or even up wire-netting. In the latter case it has to be tied into position, for its clingers are not really sufficient to support the stems when carrying those heavy fruits.

Soil and manuring If the crop can follow one which has been liberally manured, there is no special cultivation to be done. As much organic matter as possible should, however, be incorporated, and, in addition, bone meal should be applied at 3 ozs per square yard and wood ashes at 3 ozs per square yard. (For those who don't mind using chemical fertilizers, sulphate of potash at 1 oz to the square yard may be added.)

Seed-sowing It is usual to sow seeds in 3 inch pots in a greenhouse, early in April, and the plants are thus quite ready to be put out into open ground towards the end of May.

Those who have no greenhouse may sow the seed in frames or in a little pocket of specially prepared soil outside where the plants are to grow.

The little pockets should be prepared with plenty of organic matter, and an upturned glass jamjar should be placed over them in order to help germination and to give the seedlings some protection when they come through.

It is inadvisable to sow the seed much before the first week of May.

Planting Where numbers of marrows are to be grown, the plants should be put in 3 ft apart in the rows, and if there are to be numbers of rows, the rows should be 4 ft apart. Bush marrows are preferable under this system. Trailers grown under such conditions have to be kept pinched back. It is on the rubbish heap and the odd corner that they may be allowed to ramble as they like.

General cultivation Hoeing should be done regularly, and top dressings given of grass mowings or rotted leaves, etc., during June.

Harvesting Marrows should be cut when they are young and tender, for then the plants will produce a heavier crop. Regular cutting may treble a crop.

Varieties Roller; a white, trailing type bearing a large, smooth marrow with no rib or neck. Bush-shaped green; bears medium sized fruits. Bush-shaped white; similar to former, but creamy-white. Zucchini; early and very heavy cropper.

9 Ensuring plenty of salads and herbs

It is always necessary to be able to produce a palatable food, and the growing of a few herbs for the purpose of flavouring cannot be considered a waste of space. Correct seasoning can make a dish very appetizing, even though it is not the normal fare of the consumer. There is no need to grow more than three or four herbs at a time, and this chapter concentrates on a few only. They are all of them quite easy to cultivate, and can be used all the year round.

All of them are quite easy to dry and store away in packets or jars. If the fresh leaves are brought in and laid on butter-muslin (or cheese-cloth, as it is sometimes called) on a shelf, in the oven, with the oven door open, it will be found that they dry slowly and yet keep their colour and flavour. The oven should not be a hot one.

They can also be dried lying on butter-muslin on a board or tray in front of the fire, but if this method is adopted, a longer period must elapse before they are ready. After drying it is quite easy to powder them before storing.

Salads, too, are useful, because they are eaten fresh, and are therefore rich in vitamin content. Lettuce, for instance, is very high in vitamin A and C, quite high in vitamin B1, and contains vitamin B2 as well. It is true that the lettuce contains 95 per cent water, but even that is less than the marrow, and about the same as the runner bean and the Spanish onion. It does, however, contain 2 per cent carbohydrates, and in these is equal to the celery, radish and perpetual spinach, and is richer than the Spanish onion and cucumber.

Lettuce, too, contains lime and iron, which are necessary to balance the excess phosphates found in cereal and meat foods.

Even mustard and cress are useful, for their calorific content per pound stands at 125, and the carbohydrate content at 4. Tomatoes are very useful indeed, since they are rich in vitamins, as will be seen from the chart at the end of the book.

CHIVES

This has been described as a baby salad onion. It grows in a little clump, the clump spreading as the year proceeds. Chives can be pulled or cut at any time of the year, and they make it possible to have the subtle onion flavouring all the year round.

The plants make a very nice edging to a border, and when growing look something like thrift. They will do well under quite dry conditions. Plant in October or April in a nice sunny position.

Propagation is effected by division in the spring.

LETTUCE

It is possible, by careful management and by the use of continuous cloches or frames, to ensure having crisp hearts of lettuce all the year round.

Two groups are grown, the cos and the cabbage.

Lettuces can be cooked as well as eaten raw, and this is a useful way of using up any that are starting to go to seed, or for some other reason are not fit for salad purposes. The leaves and hearts should be boiled in a little water until tender. This takes about forty minutes. The water should then be drained off, the leaves chopped up roughly, and returned to the pan, plus a little butter and gravy or a few drops of meat extract.

Soil and manuring When preparing the soil for lettuce, much finely divided organic matter should be forked into the top 3 ins or so. This helps to ensure that moisture is retained during the warmer months. Compost should be forked in at the rate of one good barrow-load to 12 square yards, and at the same time add 2 ozs of meat and bone meal or a good fish manure, and $\frac{1}{2}$ oz of sulphate of potash, or better still 2 ozs of wood ashes per square yard.

Seed-sowing The man who wishes to have lettuce all the year round should be prepared to sow a thimbleful of lettuce seed throughout the spring and summer right up to the end of August.

The principal sowings will be made from the beginning of March to the middle of April, and it is possible to sow at three-weekly intervals from this time until August. The plants raised from these sowings may either be allowed to grow where they are sown, or may be thinned out and transplanted to further borders. The secret of success with lettuce transplanting is to do it when they are just big enough to handle.

The drills for the earliest sowings are usually 6 ins apart, and as soon as the young seedlings appear, they are thinned out to 2 ins apart. The sowings that are made in the open for growing where they are sown should be in rows 1 ft apart, the plants being thinned to 10 ins apart.

During the third week in August in the south, and about the second week in the north, seed should be sown on a warm seed bed, and the plants thus raised put out in rows 1 ft apart and 10 ins apart in the rows. These are left outside over winter. Again, it is possible to sow the rows where the lettuces are to grow, and to thin the plants out to 5 ins before the winter sets in, and to 10 ins apart in the spring. They should be ready for use in May and early June.

Frames Those who have frames may make a sowing about the second week of October in the north, and the third week in the south, in rows 10 ins apart. The seedlings are thinned out to 9 ins apart, and the plants are left in the frames to winter, being given air on every possible occasion.

Winter sowing Lettuce seed may also be sown in November, the compost being a light one, and rich in organic matter. The soil in which the lettuces are sown should be thoroughly soaked after seed-sowing, and if this is done there should be no need to water after the plants are through.

Cloches Those who have continuous cloches or square Access frames will find them particularly valuable for sowings made during the middle of August or the middle of October, for it is possible by using them to obtain lettuces up to the end of the year in the case of August sowings, and for an early spring supply in the case of those sown in October.

It is usually unnecessary to cover lettuce with cloches in the summer, but they are of great value from August onwards. The rows should run east and west, and then the sun's rays strike the glass at the right angle, and therefore have greater powers of penetration.

Transplanting As has already been said, lettuces should be transplanted early and firmly. They should be handled carefully, for they are tender and easily damaged. They should be transplanted quickly, for their roots dry out quickly, but should not be planted deeply, for then they go 'peaky'.

General cultivation Keep the hoe going between the rows whenever necessary. It is not advisable to go on the land in the winter if the soil is wet, but, whenever the soil is warm enough, surface cultivation will do a great deal of good.

Cos lettuces do not heart as easily as cabbage varieties, and for this reason they are often tied round the middle with raffia when they have made three-quarters of their growth. Cos lettuces, too, seem to need far more moisture, and so should be watered regularly if the season is a dry one. It is usual only to make spring and summer sowings of the cos varieties.

Varieties Cabbage:

Spring sowing: All the Year Round; a good variety for a hot summer and will stand a good long time before going to seed. Webbs Wonderful; the curly, crinkly-leaved lettuce that is much liked for its crispness.

August sowing: Arctic King; exceedingly hardy and matures quickly. Cheshunt Early Giant; produces good hearts and when forced is ready for use in February and March. Kloek; is excellent for sowing under glass for spring cutting.

Varieties Cos:

Summer sowing: Buttercrunch; crisp and succulent and remains in good table condition long after most other varieties have become bitter or run to seed. Little Gem; is mid-way between cabbage and cos, and for sheer flavour has no equal.

Winter sowing: Winter Density; large very dark green with solid hearts.

MUSTARD AND CRESS

One of the most easily grown crops, though on certain soils it 'damps off' easily. In such cases the soil should be sterilized before using, by heating it to 210°F for twenty minutes. Sowing the seed on damp sacking laid on soil is a good idea.

Cress should be sown three days before mustard. It is usually convenient to sow in boxes, and these should be kept in the dark for a few days to ensure long stems. They should be brought out into the light again five days before cutting, to get the green colouring matter back into the leaves.

They are cut off with scissors when required, as pulling them up by the roots is apt to make the salad gritty.

The best variety for sowing is the white mustard. After the middle of March mustard and cress may be sown outside, first of all in a south border, and then in a north border. Successive sowings may be made until the middle of September.

RADISHES

With the introduction of new varieties the old idea about indigestion does not hold good, and especially so when the roots are compost grown. They are one of the quickest vegetables to grow. The seed is cheap and gives a big return.

Soil and manuring Radishes do not need deep soil. They will grow equally well on clays and sands, providing they are properly prepared. The main thing is to see that the soil is not lumpy and that it is rich in organic matter. 4 ozs of meat and bone meal and, for those who don't mind using chemicals, ½ oz sulphate of potash should be raked in. The best thing is to use 3 ozs of wood ashes.

Seed-sowing Radish seed should always be sown thinly. Broadcasting is possible, but it is better to sow in rows 6 ins apart, the drills being ½ inch deep.

The soil should always be made firm after sowing, as this ensures firm, crisp radishes.

It is possible to make a sowing outside as late as December in a special sheltered place. The bed should be a raised one. After sowing, the bed should be covered with straw to a depth of 4 ins, but immediately the seed has germinated, the straw should be taken off, so as to allow the plants to grow in the light. If there is any sign of frost or snow, the straw should be replaced to give protection. It may be removed when the weather is warm.

The next sowing should be in a warm, dry border in February, this being covered with litter as before.

Further sowings may be made once a fortnight or every three weeks from the middle of March to the beginning of September. The summer sowings prefer a cool, shady place.

Radishes are very useful in an emergency, for they can be grown as an intercrop between the rows of other vegetables, such as peas, beans, carrots, etc. They may also be sown in rows of vegetables, like asparagus, parsnips and seakale, whose seeds germinate slowly.

Varieties French Breakfast; bright scarlet, white tipped, quick growth, mild and very tender. Scarlet Globe; brilliant red, flesh white and of delicate flavour. Long White Icicle; long, white and tapering, early and crisp. China Rose; long, blunt ended roots with slight thickening at base, hardy and exceptionally valuable for winter use.

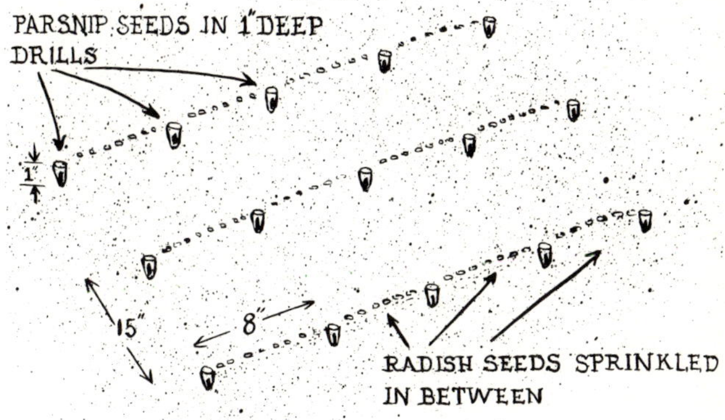

Intercropping as carried out in the vegetable garden

RADISHES – WINTER

Few people know about the excellent winter radishes. They grow large and look more like turnips. They can be used in salads, or may be boiled and used as a vegetable. The roots may be left in the ground and dug up as desired.

Sowing The seed should be sown in July in the north, and August in the south. The drills should be 9 ins apart, and when the plants are 2 ins high they should be thinned out to 6 ins apart.

Varieties Black Spanish Long; has black skin, but firm white flesh. Black Spanish Round; similar to former, but round.

TOMATOES

Tomatoes can be grown in the open as well as under cloches or in glasshouses or frames. In the open they are excellent grown against a south wall, and in fact in any sunny position. They need, too, plenty of air.

Soil and manuring The soil should be cultivated, and if there is any fear that it is badly drained, the tomatoes should be planted on ridges, with the compost below.

Well made compost should be forked in also, and in addition: bone meal; and, during wet seasons, sulphate of potash should be applied at 1 oz per square yard late in June and late in July – or, better still, wood ashes.

Seed-sowing Those without greenhouses will be well advised to purchase sturdy, short-jointed plants about 8 ins high. These may be put in the ground about the end of May or the beginning of June.

Planting The hole should not be too deep, and the grower's aim should be to bury the roots so that they are covered with ½ inch new soil. Firm planting is essential and, to prevent the plants from being damaged, they should be staked immediately with a bamboo.

Where there are a number of plants to be grown in a row, two good posts should be put at each end and a wire stretched tightly between them. The plants can then be tied up to the wires where they should go.

General cultivation Directly the plants are in land should be hoed over to produce a loose surface and this hoeing should be continued throughout the season.

Side-shoots should be removed as they grow so as to restrict the plants to one or two main stems. As new growth takes place, so must tying be attended to, and, when tying, a space should be left for the stem to swell.

During the first week of August it is advisable to stop the plants, that is, to pinch off the growing point. Large numbers of side-shoots will push out as a result of the stopping, and these must be removed immediately.

In order to allow the sun to get at the ripening fruit, whole leaves may be removed here and there right back to the main stem. It is better to do this than to cut back a large number of leaves by half.

Spraying as a preventive against the potato blight may be necessary in wet years as advised for potatoes.

Harvesting The fruit should be picked as it ripens. It is fairly easy to continue the ripening of the fruit indoors, if necessary, on the window-ledge. Any fruits that have not ripened by the end of September must be removed, and be ripened in the house.

Varieties Histon Cropper; produces a fantastically large crop which ripens very quickly and is highly resistant to blight. Outside Girl; heavy cropper of excellent quality.

WATERCRESS

Few people realise that watercress can be grown without water. A watercress bed can be made almost any time in the spring. A shady situation is best, and a dark, damp corner where nothing else will grow is ideal.

A simple plan is to dig a trench 2 ft deep and 2 or 3 ft wide, and place in the bottom of it a 9 inch layer of composted manure or other similar organic substitute. This should be given a thorough soaking, and the trench should be left for 14 days or so, two or three bucketsful of water being given to the trench every day.

Before planting, 3 or 4 ins of good soil should be placed over the manure and pressed firm. The young plants should be set out 8 ins square.

If seed is to be sown directly into the trench, three or four seeds may be sown at each 'station' 8 ins apart, the seedlings being thinned down to one or two if they all germinate. During germination the trench should be kept dark by covering it with old sacks or matting laid across a framework, bamboos, or poles.

The soil should never be allowed to get dry, and should be watered every day through a fine rose, unless it rains. When the young plants are rooted, the leading shoots should be pinched out, and the plants will thus bush out. Later, if there is any sign of the plants flowering, they should be cut back and allowed to start again.

In order to keep up a constant supply of young plants, it is better to make three or four small beds rather than one large one. The stems that are pulled off are then fresher and more palatable.

HERBS

Mint:

The Spearmint is the variety which is most used for mint sauce. It is propagated by means of division of roots. The roots may be cut up into pieces an inch long, and these can be planted 6 ins apart in any suitable situation. Mint will grow almost anywhere.

A damp situation is best, and to ensure freedom from rust and the maximum crop a new bed should be made in March each year.

Where rust is very bad the roots should be washed before planting or they may be put in warm water at a temperature at 110°F for twenty minutes. After washing, the underground stems should be trimmed so as to remove the little roots.

Parsley:

Parsley makes a good edging plant. It should always be sown thinly if good rows are to result. Thinning should be carried out early to prevent the plants from crowding.

Parsley will grow in almost any soil. A sowing may be made in March for the summer and in June for the winter. If only one sowing is to be made, this is best done in May. (It is very fond of growing near roses.)

If one or two rows are to be sown, they should be 1 ft

apart. In all cases the plants should be thinned out first of all to 3 ins apart, and finally to 6 ins apart. The thinnings may be transplanted to other rows if necessary.

If the plants tend to get coarse, they should be cut down, and the young growth that results will be green and tender.

Varieties Moss Curled; a useful variety for general purposes. New Dark Green Winter; dark emerald-green colour, and stands the winter better than any other variety.

Sage:

The broad-leaved green sage is the most valuable. It is better to buy plants than to sow seed. Cuttings may be taken with a piece of the older wood attached in April or May, and may be rooted in a sandy medium.

The plants should be put out in rows 2 ft apart and 1 ft apart in the rows. After planting they should be hoed regularly, and if they show signs of flowering, the flowering-stems should be removed.

Thyme:

Either common thyme or lemon thyme may be grown. Both make an effective edging and can be used in dry borders where parsley will not grow readily. Common thyme may be raised from seed-sowings, but it is better to propagate lemon thyme by division of roots in March and April, or by cuttings in September.

The rows should be 2 ft apart, and the plants 18 ins apart in the rows.

10 Unusual vegetables

There are a number of unusual vegetables that a number of people have never heard of. Many of them are rich in vitamins and high in calorific value. They are no more difficult to grow than the ordinary kinds, and they do provide an important appetising change from the eternal potatoes and cabbage.

CELERIAC

This grows like a turnip and tastes just like the heart of celery. It is excellent when sliced into salad or when cooked. It is easy to grow and has not got to be earthed up or blanched like celery. Another great advantage is that the vegetable will keep for six months after it is fully grown.

Seed-sowing The seed should be sown as for self-bleaching celery, the seedlings being pricked out into frames when large enough. The young plants should be put out in May or early June in rows 1 ft apart, and the plants being 1 ft apart in the rows.

General cultivation Celeriac is a gross feeder, and should be grown on land that has been well manured. One good barrow-load of well-rotted compost may be applied over 12 square yards. In addition a good fish manure should be raked into the top 3 or 4 ins at 4 or 5 ozs to the square yard, while organic fertilizers may be given as well, as advised for carrots.

The rows should be hoed, and if possible should be watered once a week from the end of June onwards if the weather is dry. Liquid manure may be added to each watering if the land is poor.

When planting, the side-growths should be removed. A fortnight before the roots are to be lifted the soil should be hoed up to the foliage to cause the upper part of the root to become blanched. The celeriac may be dug up and stored in soil in a shed, or in a clamp as advised for potatoes. In the south of England it is possible to leave the roots outside and cover them up during the very hard frosts with soil or bracken.

SQUASHES

These form a very valuable food, for, after harvesting, the large, marrow-like fruits may be stored in a shed, and portions may be cut off as desired, for use throughout the winter. They should be grown in the same way as marrows, either being made to climb up wire-netting or a fence, or being grown on the rubbish-heap or on the flat.

Seed-sowing The plants should be raised in frames or under glass from seed sown in pots any time during April or early May. Two seeds are usually sown per 3 inch pot, and if both grow, the weakest is removed.

It is possible, also, to sow the seeds where the plants are to grow, but this results in later cropping.

Slugs like these plants and should be kept at bay with Draza pellets.

General cultivation Any old fermenting material, such as grass mowings, may be buried in a heap so as to give the young plants a hot-bed underneath. This heating of the soil gets them growing quickly from the start.

Harvesting The squashes may be harvested directly they are of sufficient size, or they can be left till they are full grown, so that they may be hung up for use during the winter.

Varieties Hubbard Squash; should not be eaten until September or October. Will keep until February. Perhaps the most useful winter variety. Should be steamed, or the pieces baked in their own skin, and then mashed with butter or margarine. Makes a delicious soup, made up with milk, and a delicious pie.

Banana Squash; has the consistency of a banana, with a delicious flavour. Is really a summer sort, but will keep into the winter.

Acorn Squash; a small variety. Should be cooked whole, one being served to each person. Is lovely stuffed with meat or ham.

Golden Scallop Squash; is quite round, and is excellent served with bacon in the morning. Can be kept for use all the year round. Is first class for the winter months.

PUMPKINS

May be grown in exactly the same way as squashes or marrows. Very useful because they keep. They have a flavour distinctly their own.

MARROW, PUMPKIN AND SQUASH TIPS

It is sometimes necessary to pinch back the growing tips of marrows, pumpkins or squashes and these should be saved and used in the kitchen, for they form an excellent substitute for spinach.

If marrows are grown in rows, it is often advisable to keep them pinched back, and when this is done a dual-purpose vegetable is produced.

KOHL RABI

Kohl Rabi is a very popular vegetable on the Continent. It is similar in flavour to the turnip, but is more 'nutty'. Its great advantage is that it will stand quite hard frosts, and so may be left growing in the ground until required. Furthermore, it is not so liable to clubroot disease as the turnip, and so may be used on disease-infected land.

Seed-sowing The seed may be sown any time from the second week of March till the second week of August. Those who want continuity may make a succession of sowings every three weeks. The rows should be 2 ft apart and the seedlings thinned to 3 ins apart in the early stages, and finally to 6 ins apart. The young plants pulled at this final thinning are in a fit condition to be used as a vegetable. Thus this method of thinning is important.

General cultivation When hoeing, the earth should not be drawn up to the plants, but rather away from them.

Varieties *For early work:* Earliest White; delicately flavoured. *For later sowings:* Early Purple; a winter vegetable.

WELSH ONION

This is a herbaceous perennial which came originally from Siberia. There are two types, a red and a white, but neither of them throws large bulbs, and the onions they produce always look like spring onions. It is a very hardy vegetable and one that is available all the year round. With the Welsh onion in the garden there is never any fear of not having onions for flavouring soups, salads and stews.

Seed-sowing The seed may be sown in July or August, or young plants may be obtained by the division of the old ones. Each onion plant may produce thirty or forty onion plants around it. It will grow almost anywhere.

SUGAR PEA

An excellent pea for emergency periods, for the peas are eaten pod and all. There is no need to do any shelling. The pod has a definite food value. It is advisable just to top and tail them like gooseberries, before boiling them.

Seed-sowing The seed should be sown in exactly the same way as for ordinary peas, the main sowing being made in May, in rows 4 ft apart. It grows to a height of 5 or 6 ft, and requires support of pea sticks or wire netting.

Harvesting The pods should be picked regularly while they are young and fresh. If any of the pods are allowed to get old, the plant ceases to crop heavily.

SALSIFY

A root crop which is becoming increasingly popular, even though it is still considered unusual.

It grows best on a light, loamy soil, though it will do quite well in a heavy clay, providing it has been properly prepared. It does best, perhaps, when following a crop that has been well manured the previous year. Like other root crops, it should not be grown on soil that has been recently manured.

Organic fertilizers should be applied as advised for parsnips.

Seed-sowing The seed should be sown in April, the drills being 1 ft apart and 1 inch deep. Directly the seedlings are large enough they should be thinned out, first of all to 4 ins apart, and then to 8 ins apart.

General cultivation Hoeing may be carried out within and between the rows to keep down weeds if necessary. The roots should never be cut when hoeing, or they tend to bleed.

Harvesting It should be possible to use the roots first of all during the second or third week of October, but, like parsnips, they come to no harm if left in the ground until required. They, therefore, need take up little storage room – a good point in their favour.

Varieties The best variety is Mammoth Sandwich Island.

DUTCH BEANS

Dutch beans are very valuable in an emergency, for they are very rich in protein, containing about thirteen per cent, as compared with one per cent in savoys and two per cent in potatoes. They are also rich in fat and carbohydrates, and have a calorific value of about 700 per pound.

They may be grown in exactly the same way as French beans and the beans can either be thrashed out in their green state and used as a fresh vegetable like peas or broad beans, or, if left, the seed can be dried and used as a haricot bean.

There is no difficulty at all in their cultivation, and they are of high nutritional value and keep well.

SOYA BEANS

These also may be grown in exactly the same way as French beans. They grow to a height of 2 ft.

A large number of small beans are produced which may be cooked green or left on the plants to ripen, when, after thrashing, the beans are kept dry until required. They have quite a flavour of their own.

The soya bean is perhaps even more valuable than the Dutch bean, though in this country, it does not give a heavy return in the normal summer. It is very rich in carbohydrates, protein and fat, high in calorific value, and has a low water content.

11 Growing your own fruit

It must be remembered that the growing of fruit is a far longer process than the production of vegetables. It is possible, however, to bring some fruits into bearing in a year or two years, and this chapter will deal briefly with these. Certain fruits, like strawberries and peaches, must be looked upon as luxuries and you will have to forgo them if you are short of space.

This chapter does not attempt to be a treatise on the growing of fruit in Great Britain, and those who wish for further information from me should study *Compost Fruit Growing*, published by Pelham Bros.

APPLES

For immediate cropping, apple trees should be purchased on dwarfing stocks. Malling 9 is the dwarfing stock most used, and it is most suitable for cordons or for small bush trees. Malling 2 is used principally for bush trees or, in the case of weak varieties, for cordons. It is quite a suitable stock for a small garden.

It may be advisable to purchase two or three year old trees, because these will come into cropping earlier.

The man with the small garden will naturally study the space he has available and will determine to grow the type of tree on the correct stock which will take up the minimum amount of room. The cordon seems ideal for this purpose. This is a tree with a single stem. The side growths are pruned back hard, and fruit spurs are encouraged all along the stem. It takes up very little room, and it enables the garden owner to grow a large number of varieties.

Those who do not wish to put up wires onto which the cordons are trained should grow dwarf pyramids. These are like upright cordons except that the short side branches are allowed to develop somewhat.

Bush trees are also popular, the branches being trained so that the tree is goblet-shaped. If dwarfing stocks are insisted on, early cropping bush trees can be produced.

These dwarf trees are easy to prune and spray, and are much to be preferred in an emergency to standard and half standards, which take a long time to come into cropping and need plenty of room.

It is a mistake to dig in heavy quantities of organic matter before planting apple trees (or any fruit trees, for that matter). What organic matter is used should be applied to the surface of the ground after planting, so as to give a mulching. It is a mistake, also, to plant in 'dirty' land. Once the trees are in, it is almost impossible to get rid of the roots of perennial weeds.

Apple trees may be planted any time between November and, say, the beginning of March. Autumn planting, however, is always preferable to spring planting.

There is no need to dig a deep hole for fruit trees. One 9 ins deep is sufficient, and on heavy land a hole 3 ins deep is sufficient. A hole 3 ft by 3 ft is large enough. Care should be taken not to plant the tree so deeply that the graft is buried below the ground.

The roots should be spread out evenly like the rays of the sun, and soil should be placed over them, spadeful by spadeful, and trodden down firmly. Firm but not over-firm planting is advisable. When the hole is filled, there should be a slight mound towards the centre to allow for settling down afterwards.

The cordons will be tied up to the wires provided, while for the bush trees and dwarf pyramids, stakes should be driven into the ground at an angle of about 45°. Bands of sacking should be wrapped round the stems of the trees at the point where they are to be tied to the stake and they should be tied with tarred string. It is most necessary to stake trees, to keep them firm, so that a good root-system may be formed quickly.

Cordons may be planted in rows 5 ft apart, the trees being 2 ft apart in the rows. The bush trees and dwarf pyramids on the type 9 may be planted as close as 8 ft and on type 2 stock as close as 10 ft square.

Manuring Apply a fish manure or a seaweed manure at 3 ozs to the square yard, plus wood ashes at 4 ozs to the square yard.

Pruning To get the trees into cropping immediately, it is better to carry out little or no pruning than to cut them hard back. A certain amount of knifing might be done just to keep the bush open and to cut back the laterals (or side growths in the case of the cordons). The dwarf pyramids would have to be pruned in a special manner, and my book on pruning goes into detail on this subject.

Varieties It is always advisable to have varieties that will keep so that the food supply can be kept up during the winter months. The following list has, therefore, been very carefully compiled, and includes only varieties that will crop early, take up little room when grafted on to dwarfing stocks, and will keep well.

Eaters	*Cookers*
Ellison's Orange	Lane's Prince Albert
Laxton's Superb	Edward VII
Upton Pyne	Encore

It may be convenient to grow dual-purpose apples (varieties to either eat or cook), and the following seem to fit the bill admirably, bearing in mind the reasons for the previous choice of apples:

Allington Pippin	Rival
Barnack Beauty	Charles Ross
Herring's Pippin	Wagoner

PEARS

It should be possible to grow one or two pears, either for keeping and stewing or for dessert purposes. The trees should be purchased on either the Malling A or Malling C stocks, which bring the trees into cropping early.

Pears are not, perhaps, as useful as apples, for they blossom much earlier and are more likely to be damaged by frost.

Manuring As for apples, except that on dry soil some organic matter should be given as a top dressing, especially where growth shows a decline.

Purchase of trees, planting, pruning, etc. Treatment as advised for apples applies.

Pollination The pollination problem of pears is acute. Most of the varieties are self-sterile – that is, they need the pollen of another variety flowering at the same time to cause the blossoms to set and produce fruit. It is suggested, therefore, that only self-fertile varieties should be grown.

Eaters	*Cookers*
Conference	Uvedale's St. Germain
Hessle	
Williams Bon Chretien	

As Williams have to be sprayed with lime-sulphur and dusted with copper lime if scab is to be kept down, and as Hessle throws such a small pear, it would probably be better to concentrate on Conference and Uvedale's.

PLUMS

Plums like richer soil than apples, but good drainage is less important. The common mussel may be compared to the type 9 stock in apples, and is suitable for bush trees and for bringing into early cropping varieties that are normally rather slow.

Manuring The trees should receive regular mulchings (top dressings) of farmyard manure of a suitable organic substitute during the summer, and organic matter should be forked in during the winter at the rate of one barrow-load to 6 square yards. Meat and bone meal can be used in addition at the rate of 4 ozs to the square yard and wood ash at 4 ozs to the square yard.

Garden lime should be applied at $\frac{1}{2}$ lb to the square yard to the surface of the ground in January, but it might not be necessary to apply lime again for three or four years.

Planting For quick results bush plums are recommended on stems 3 ft high. They should be planted 15 ft apart. It is possible to plant any time between late October and late February.

Pruning The end one year old growths, or leaders as they are called, on young trees may be pruned quite hard so that a good strong framework may be built up.

To obviate attacks of silver-leaf, it is best to prune plums in the spring, and to do sufficient so that the trees may be kept open. All pruning cuts on plums should be painted over afterwards with a thick white-lead paint.

Varieties Most varieties of plums are self-sterile, and, to save planting pollinators, it is best to concentrate on a few self-fertile varieties. The following crop heavily.

Eaters	*Cookers*
Victoria	Czar
	Giant Prune
	Pershore
	Purple Pershore

GOOSEBERRIES

Gooseberries can be bottled and kept, as can of course, plums and damsons. They do, however, require a large amount of sugar. They will grow on almost any soil, and if three year old bushes are obtained, they will crop immediately.

Manuring A good barrow-load of composted manure or a suitable organic substitute should be applied to the soil surface to every twelve bushes in January or February. This may be followed in April by the addition of seaweed manure at 4 ozs to the square yard. Wood ashes are excellent for gooseberries at 6 ozs to the square yard.

Planting The gooseberry bush should be obtained growing on a 6 inch leg. This leg allows for ease of cultivation and prevents suckers coming up from the roots. It is better to plant before the turn of the year than in the new year.

Pruning The end one year old growths or leaders will need cutting back to half for the first three or four years so as to form a strong framework from which the other branches may be produced. Once the tree is established, it is only necessary to keep open the centre of the bush and to remove crowding or rubbing branches, together with any that are near the ground.

Picking and protection To get the best results, picking should be begun at Whitsun and the berries thinned in this way. The largest berries should be picked first, with the result that the others get a chance of swelling. A picking over once a fortnight should fit the bill.

In gardens where there are numbers of birds, it is necessary to protect the bushes in winter from bud pecking by twining black cotton in and among the branches.

Varieties The best bottling varieties are: Lancashire Lad, a red; Cousin's Seedling, a yellow; Careless, a green and Langley Gage, a white.

Lancashire Lad is probably the pick of these, for it is the heaviest cropper and perhaps the strongest grower.

BLACKCURRANTS

Blackcurrants make excellent jam and can be bottled or canned. They succeed on all kinds of soils and will put up with wetter soil conditions than any other fruit.

Manuring Heavy dressings of compost should be applied each autumn, as a top dressing. In addition, fish manure or seaweed manure should be given at the rate of 4 ozs per bush. In January a further feed may be given at 2 ozs to the square yard.

Planting A blackcurrant bush should not be grown on a leg, but the branches should arise from ground level. Bushes should be two or three years old when planted.

Pruning As the bulk of the fruit is borne on the previous year's wood, care should be taken to remove one or two branches bodily every year, so as to keep the bush full of new growth.

Blackcurrants should not be planted in situations where they are likely to be damaged by frost. The situation should be sheltered, for many of the varieties rely on insect visitation for pollination, and insects will not work in windswept situations.

Varieties The following varieties do not depend on insect pollination, and are good growers and heavy croppers: Baldwin (Hilltop Strain), small berries; Wellington 30, mid-season large berries; Westwick Choice, medium firm berries ripen late; Mendip Cross, fairly large berries, very early.

BLACKBERRIES AND LOGANBERRIES

It is possible to grow a blackberry or loganberry in an odd corner that is not suitable for any other fruit. They can both of them be trained against fences or along wires, and they can be grown against the house. They are both heavy croppers, useful for bottling or canning, and excellent for jam.

Manuring Good compost should be applied as a top dressing in May each year. In addition, a fish manure should be put on in the autumn at the rate of 3 ozs per square yard.

Planting If they are to be trained along wires, against the fence, or against trellis-work, they will need to be 12 to 15 ft apart.

Pruning The old canes should be cut down to the ground when they have finished fruiting, and the new canes tied up in their place.

Harvesting To ensure maggot-free berries, the flowers should be dusted with derris when they are starting to open. A second dusting should be given a week later. It should be possible to pick the blackberries from August to mid-October, and the loganberries just before they are fully ripe.

Varieties *Blackberries:* Thornless Evergreen; fruits July to September.

Loganberries: Thornless Logans; fruits July to September.

RASPBERRIES

Buy virus free canes from a firm like Rivers, Sawbridgeworth, Herts.

Planting Plant one year old canes in November 1 ft apart in the row – with the next row 6 ft away.

Manuring Give plenty of powdery compost in May each year. Apply also a fish or seaweed manure each October at 3 ozs to the square yard.

Pruning Cut down to ground level the canes that have fruited immediately all the berries have been picked.

Training Tie up the canes to a wire stretched tightly from posts at either end of the row.

Harvesting Pick the raspberries the moment they are ripe.

Varieties Mallery Jewel; the heaviest cropper, fruit of a superb flavour. Norfolk Giant; the best late fruiting variety.

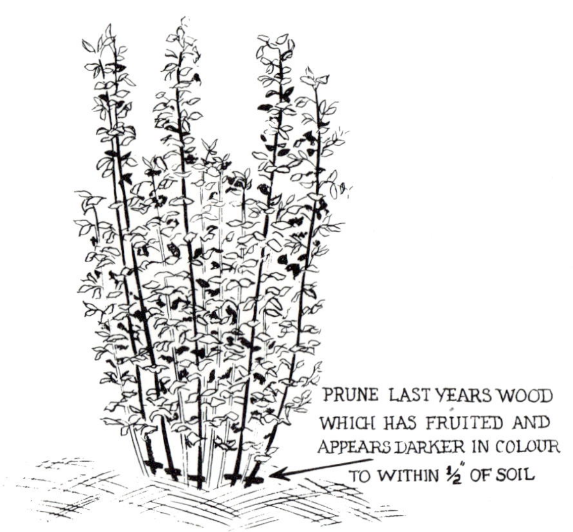

Raspberry pruning

BRIEF FRUIT-GROWING HINTS

The successful grower will do everything possible to prevent the spread of pests and diseases by burning infected prunings and dead wood. He will not allow refuse to collect in any odd corners of the garden.

All the trees and bushes should be sprayed each February with a white oil wash, using a five per cent solution. The spraying should be done on a fine day.

Fruit should always be gathered at the right time. When apples, for instance, are picked too early, they tend to shrivel; if picked too late, they will not store and keep.

The utmost care should be taken in handling fruits and in placing them in the containers. Apples and pears should be gathered by lifting them up with the palm of the hand when the stalks should come away from the spur quite easily.

Apples and pears, too, can be bruised if the container is rough. A basket should always be lined and padded with felt. The fruit should be placed in the container, and not dropped in.

In some cases – for instance, with gooseberries – it is necessary to pick fruits before they are ripe. Late varieties of apples and pears may very often be left on the tree until the leaves start to fall.

In the case of varieties of apples, the following is usually the order in which picking should be carried out:

The first week in October: Charles Ross, Herring's Pippin, Rival, Lane's Prince Albert.

Second week of October: Barnack Beauty, Encore.

Third week of October: Upton Pyne, Wagoner.

Fourth week of October: Edward VII.

If the apples and pears are to be stored, they should be allowed to sweat outside for a week or so in suitable containers. The storehouse should be so constructed that the temperature keeps at round about 40°F. Air should circulate between the fruits, so that the store does not heat up. The store should be absolutely clean and not too dry.

It is possible to convert a good cellar, a first class attic, or a barn into a 'fruit-house', and in emergency it is possible to keep apples by putting a thick layer of straw on the floor and another thick layer around the walls. The apples can then be laid on the straw, piled up 3 ft deep. The straw helps to give the necessary insulation.

12 Pests and diseases and their control by natural methods

Pests and diseases are never as serious on land that has been supplied with sufficient organic matter as they are on soil which is fast reverting to desert conditions owing to lack of humus. It is important, therefore, to see that the ground is given adequate supplies of composted manure or some efficient substitute.

In addition, soil that is lacking in potash often grows plants that are soft leaved and these are more likely to be attacked by mildews and rusts as well as aphides and capsids. The application of sulphate of potash each season will help to make up deficiencies.

Plants that are crowded grow long, lanky and weedy, and are, therefore, more vulnerable to many more ills than are plants that are growing healthily. Weeds should be kept down, as they act as alternative host-plants to the pests and diseases. The land should be properly drained, and lime should be applied regularly to prevent the soil from becoming acid.

The sowing of seed and the planting out should always be done at the right time. Late sowings may be attacked by pests, and early sowings damaged by weather conditions.

Directly the leaves of a plant turn yellow, and are useless, they should be removed as they are potential homes of a fungus disease.

PESTS THAT WILL ATTACK VARIOUS VEGETABLES

Aphides

Varieties of these are known as greenfly, blue bug, blackfly, or the 'blight'. Actually they are a very large family of plant lice which attack all members of the cabbage family, as well as carrots, peas, beans, etc. They multiply at an extraordinary rate, and should be controlled in the early stages. They are sucking insects, and often cause the leaves to curl.

Control: They can usually be controlled if derris is applied forcefully either as a dust or a spray. Derris is non-poisonous, so that it may be used at any time. In the case of badly curled leaves, a nicotine spray is preferable.

Flea-beetles

Flea-beetles are small and are generally black or dark grey. They damage young plants as they are coming through, and are particularly bad in the case of turnips, carrots and radishes and all members of the cabbage family. They will attack the leaves of older plants.

They hop quickly and hide themselves. Large numbers on a plant may cause it to look quite black. They spend the winter in dry vegetable rubbish, and they may start attacking plants in May and continue right up to August.

Control: Hedge bottoms and other such places should be kept cleaned, and any rubbish that collects there, burned.

Where the pest is common, the seeds of all the cabbage family should be wetted with paraffin, using it at the rate of $\frac{1}{8}$ pint to $\frac{1}{2}$ lb of seed. The seed should be dried over night and sown the next day. Just before the plants are through, a good dusting may be given with derris as it is at this stage that the beetles often do the greatest harm. Further dustings may be necessary at weekly intervals until the plants are quite free.

Caterpillars

Different kinds of caterpillars may be found on vegetables, the most common being the green caterpillars of the Cabbage White Butterfly, found on members of the cabbage family.

Control: Caterpillars may easily be controlled by spraying or dusting with derris.

Slugs

Slugs are a regular pest in the vegetable garden, and seem a particular enemy of potatoes and celery. They feed above ground during the night and below ground during the day. Their eggs are white, translucent and look like glistening little balls.

Control: Birds do not like the colour blue. Draza pellets which are blue may therefore be used for slug control without danger to birds. Giving the soil a top dressing of sedge peat makes it impossible for the slugs to move about on the soil. *Another method* entails forking the land in the autumn or winter, with a mixture of equal parts of finely powdered copper sulphate and hydrated lime at 1 oz per square yard. This mixture kills any creature with which it comes into contact, but chemists fear that *continued* use of copper sulphate may injure the soil. A little sprinkling of this mixture should be made completely round the garden on the surface of the soil to deter slugs from migrating into your garden from other parts.

Wireworms

This is the grub of the click beetle, and it may live in the soil for four or five years before turning into a beetle.

Control: There is no really good method of control. Whizzed naphthalene may be forked in at the rate of $1\frac{1}{2}$ ozs per square yard three or four weeks before sowing seed or planting a crop. This usually drives away the wireworm.

PESTS THAT ATTACK SPECIAL CROPS

Cabbage-root Fly

This will attack the stems of plants just below the ground level and burrow into the roots also. It is a serious pest of cauliflowers, sprouts, cabbages and the like. It should not be confused with the turnip gall-weevil maggot, which will be found inside a gall or blister, and is found only in the autumn.

Control: Make a tarred felt disc say 3 ins by 3 ins. Slit it down one side to the middle so that the disc may be placed around the base of the stem of the plant – at soil level. Alternatively, grow garlic in between the rows of cabbages and the like or water a garlic solution around the plant – immediately after planting.

Carrot Fly

A small, shiny, bottle-green fly which lays its eggs near the surface of the ground along the rows of carrots. The larvae burrow down to the base of the root and burrow into this. The trouble is often first noticed when the crop is thinned.

Control: Apply whizzed naphthalene at 1 oz to the yard run just before thinning, and again ten days afterwards.

The thinned carrots should be removed and burnt, and the soil compressed to prevent egg-laying and the movement of larvae.

As a preventative, always grow onions in between carrots and vice versa. Thus, both the carrot fly and onion fly are kept at bay.

Celery Fly or Celery-leaf Miner

The fly lays her eggs on the undersides of the leaves, and the maggots that hatch out make their way in between the upper and lower skins of the leaves. Whitish looking blisters are thus formed. The attack first takes place in the seedling stage, but is not often noticed at that time.

Control: See that the young plants are free from the pest by spraying regularly with nicotine and soft soap (the formula is ½ oz liquid nicotine to a 2½ gallon bucket of water plus a teaspoonful of a liquid detergent). When in the trenches, spray early in June, again with nicotine, giving several soakings at ten day intervals. A third brood may be expected early in September.

Onion Fly

Similar in its behaviour to the carrot fly. The first attack usually takes place some time in May.

Control: Whizzed naphthalene should be used at the rate of 1 oz per yard run, just before thinning and again ten days later. (See carrot fly.)

VEGETABLE DISEASES

Club root

This disease, known as 'Finger-and-Toe' or 'Anbury', will attack the roots of any member of the cabbage family. The root swells and becomes knotted and distorted. The swellings contain rotted, evil-smelling material. The plants are dwarfed, look sickly, and never come to anything.

Control: Put half a 'clove' of garlic into each hole at planting time and the Plasmodium is kept away and so club root does not usually occur. Club root is always worse on acid soil, so see that the land is well limed.

Celery Leaf Spot or Blight

The leaves of celery turn brown in patches and little black spots may appear on the patches. In severe cases the whole leaf may wither and the plants may be ruined. The first sign of the disease occurs in July, but earlier attacks have been known in the south.

Control: The plants should be sprayed three times, once a fortnight, from the end of June onwards. Bordeaux mixture should be used and both the upper and lower sides of the leaves should be covered. In wet years four or five further applications may be advisable.

The seedsman should be asked to give a guarantee that the seeds he supplies have been treated with formaldehyde so that the fungus on the seed coat has been destroyed.

Potato Blight

Potato leaves are attacked by this disease, and dark green blotches of irregular shape will appear. These quickly turn brown and almost black. Under warm, damp conditions they may be surrounded by a delicate white mildew or mould. The disease spreads at an alarming rate, and the whole of the haulm may be killed. The spores fall to the ground and thus infest the potatoes. Dark sunken spots appear, and the affected tubers soon become rotten and useless.

Control: The haulm should be sprayed with Bordeaux mixture directly there is any sign of the trouble. The first spraying is usually done in July. Several sprayings may be necessary in a wet season. Compost grown potatoes are seldom attacked by blight, at least not in July and August as a general rule.

Potato Scab

Common scab is a disease which affects the tubers, causing brown, corky spots to appear. Attacks are more common on soils rich in lime and in gravelly or sandy soil.

Control: Grass mowings, fresh leaves or spent hops should be used to fill up the trenches where the potatoes are to grow. Lawn mowings are particularly valuable. Lime, soot or ashes should never be applied. Peelings from scab potatoes should not be dug into the ground, unless they have been properly rotted down with calcium cyanamide.

RECIPES FOR INSECTICIDES AND FUNGICIDES

Derris

This may be bought as a dust or as a powder to mix up with water for spraying. $\frac{1}{4}$ lb derris is usually dissolved in 12 gallons of water. If the manufacturer has not added soap in the preparation, $\frac{1}{2}$ lb soft soap should be stirred in.

Derris is not poisonous to human beings or animals, but is fatal to insects. It should not be used near ponds or streams, as it will also kill fish.

Derris should always be kept in a sealed container. It should be used fresh, and should be obtained with a rotenone content of at least two per cent.

Nicotine

This is generally used as a spray, though nicotine dusts can be purchased. Nicotine is always most effective when used on a warm, sunny day.

The formula is: 1 oz nicotine, 1 lb soft soap, to 10 gallons of water.

The plants should be soaked thoroughly with the spray, directing it both to the under surface and upper surface of the leaves.

N.B. Nicotine is a *poison*, and should be kept locked up when not in use.

Bordeaux Mixture

For celery use the following formula: $1\frac{1}{2}$ lb garden lime, 1 lb finely powdered copper sulphate, to 10 gallons of water.

For potatoes use: 1 lb 6 ozs hydrated lime, 1 lb 6 ozs powdered copper sulphate, to 10 gallons of water.

It is best to dissolve the crystals of copper sulphate overnight in a wooden, china or enamel container. This solution should then be poured into the lime in water solution in the morning.

N.B. Metal vessels should never be used with Bordeaux, because of the risk of corrosion.

13 What to do each month of the year

A certain amount of digging may be done by those who believe in cultivating soils and well rotted compost incorporated. It is a good month to clean out the hedge bottoms and to burn all diseased material.

Broccoli Don't forget to heel the plants over to the north, in order to save the curds.

Carrots The earliest sowing may be made in a frame over a hot-bed. Variety – Nantes Express.

Cauliflower Look at those you are over-wintering in a cold frame and remove any decaying leaves. Ventilate the frame on a nice warm day.

Lettuce May be planted out in frames over hot beds.

FEBRUARY

A sharp look-out should be kept for weeds, particularly groundsel, as this is the beginning of the seeding season.

Broad Beans Beans may be sown in boxes, and the plants raised in a cold frame ready for putting out in April.

Lettuce Plants raised in cold frames may now be planted out in sheltered borders, or in open situations to be covered with cloches. Further sowings may be made in frames for planting out later on.

Mustard and Cress Make sowings in a frame.

Parsnips Make the first sowing in the south.

Potatoes Box up the seed potatoes to sprout them.

Spinach Make a small sowing in a south border.

Turnips Make an early sowing in a warm border.

MARCH

The ground should now be in a workable condition and a good deal of seed-sowing should be possible. Frames should be ventilated more and more as the sun gains power.

Artichoke, Jerusalem Planting should be done.

Broad Beans The first outside sowing may be made, and the bean plants raised in frames may be planted out.

French Beans Seed may be sown in boxes, frames or under glass for planting out later.

Brussels Sprouts Sowings may be made outside in a seed bed.

Cabbage Sow the seeds of the summer and autumn cutting varieties. Hoe the spring cabbage and give Chilean potash nitrate.

Carrots A sowing of a stump-rooted variety may be made towards the end of the month in a warm border. Even the main crop can be sown this month in the south.

Cauliflower Raise plants of varieties like Early Snowball by making a sowing in a frame. Look over the autumn sown plants in the frames and give as much air as possible.

Chives Split up the clumps and plant in a new position. They make a good edging.

Herbs Many can be divided and replanted this month.

Lettuce Make another sowing, this time out of doors. Plant out any raised in frames.

Onions Prepare the bed and sow seeds. Transplant

any autumn sown plants if necessary.

Parsnips This is the month for northern gardeners to sow the seed.

Peas Make a sowing the first week, and another the third week. In the north, delay till the end of the month.

Radishes Make a sowing in the open.

Spinach Sow ordinary spinach and spinach beet.

Turnips Sow early varieties, towards the end of the month.

APRIL

A very busy month. Hoeing should be done if weeds are growing. Young seedlings when they come through should be thinned where necessary. Give as much air as possible to frames.

Artichoke, Jerusalem Remove all side growths, allowing only the main stem to grow.

Broad Beans Make a sowing in the open. Plant out those raised in boxes. Mulch the rows.

French Beans Make a sowing in a warm border towards the end of the month.

Runner Beans In the south make a sowing in a warm border towards the end of the month.

Beetroot Sow a main crop variety.

Broccoli Sow seeds in a seed bed. Protect against birds, flea-beetle and club root.

Brussels Sprouts Prick out plants raised last month, 4 ins apart in a seed bed. Make a main crop sowing in a seed bed.

Cabbage Sow seed of varieties to be cut in late summer or autumn. Continue to hoe spring cabbage and give

Chilean potash nitrate as advised in March.

Carrots Sow the main crop.

Cauliflower Plant the autumn sown plants. Sow seed the second week for the autumn supplies.

Herbs Sow seeds of thyme, parsley and sage.

Kohl Rabi Sow seed.

Leeks Sow seed in frames. Plants raised in the greenhouse may be planted out during the third week for early crops.

Lettuce Sow a pinch of seed once a fortnight from now onwards. Put out plants raised in frames.

Marrows Plant out seedlings raised in March and cover with cloches. Sow seed in 3-inch pots in frames.

Onions Sow main crop varieties. Put out plants raised under glass.

Peas Make sowings, if necessary and possible, once a fortnight.

Potatoes Plant main crops and earlies.

Salsify Sow seed.

Spinach Make sowings once a fortnight from now onwards if desired.

Spinach Beet Sow seed.

Turnips Make further sowings and thin out rows sown last month.

MAY

Go over the seed beds and see if there are any deficiencies, and make sowings if necessary. Thin out seedlings, pricking them out into further beds if necessary. Hoe, if necessary during the month, if weeds appear.

Broad Beans Make another sowing.

French Beans Make sowings the first, second and third week.

Runner Beans The main sowing may be made during the third week.

Beetroot Thin out earlier sown varieties and make another sowing of the main crop if necessary.

Broccoli Sow seeds of spring and summer cutting varieties (next year). Plant out any seedlings pricked out in March.

Brussels Sprouts Plant out the earliest raised plants.

Cabbage Plant summer varieties.

Carrots Thin out the earliest sowings and apply whizzed naphthalene to keep away carrot fly.

Cauliflower Make sowings outside of late hearting varieties.

Lettuce Make successional sowings. Thin out seedlings regularly and plant out if necessary. Hoe rows.

Marrows Remove cloches towards end of month. Keep plants watered regularly. Plant out those raised later during the third week.

Mustard and Cress Make sowings once a week in the open if necessary.

Peas Sow during this month for August and September use. Give earlier sowings pea sticks or wire netting for support.

Radishes Make further sowings.

Salsify Sow a row or more if desired.

Spinach Continue to make sowings.

Squashes Plant out in the open in the third week.

Turnips Make further sowings. Dust with derris to keep down turnip fly.

JUNE

Harvest many crops this month. Keep the hoe going all through the month, especially if the weather is dry. Mulch where necessary with lawn mowings and straw, and water thoroughly the plants that really need it. Always hoe and mulch as well after watering.

Keep down any weeds that appear. Thin crops out early. Put out all tender plants, like marrows. Put out many plants of the cabbage family, e.g. kale, savoys, broccoli and Brussels sprouts – whenever land becomes available.

Broad Beans Make a further sowing in the open. Dust or spray with derris to keep down black fly.

French Beans Make another sowing. Hoe between rows.

Runner Beans Provide necessary sticks. Mulch the rows towards the end of the month. Syringe the plants well in the evening in dry weather.

Beetroot Thin out the rows. Hoe regularly.

Broccoli Plant sowings made in April.

Brussels Sprouts Plant out.

Coleworts Sow this month.

Lettuce Seeds can be sown on celery ridges and thinned out. Transplant thinnings to other ground if necessary.

Onions Thin out the March and April sowings, and apply whizzed naphthalene.

Peas Sow the first early varieties again. Stock earlier sown varieties.

Potatoes Earth up potatoes when necessary.

Radishes Make a sowing once a fortnight. Protect from turnip fly by dusting with derris.

Turnips Make further sowings.

JULY

July is often a very wet month, and weeds grow apace. If it is a dry month, hoeing and mulching must be attended to.

This is the month when a start should be made with the serious composting in the wooden compost bin at least 4 ft square. Lawn mowings, old leaves of plants, hedge clippings and other ingredients listed in Chapter 2, may all be composted with an organic activator.

French Beans Sow the first week of the month for September.

Broccoli Put out any plants that are ready onto ground that is prepared.

Cabbage Make a sowing of spring cabbage seed about the third week of the month.

Carrots Make another sowing of an early variety for the autumn.

Cauliflower Plant out later sowings if necessary.

Coleworts Make a sowing for winter use.

Leeks Plant out on flat ground. Plant deeply, leaving the hole open.

Peas Hoe regularly. Continue mulching if necessary and water if dry.

Potatoes Earth up late varieties. Dig up early varieties as required.

Radishes Make further sowings.

Shallots Harvest these.

Spinach Make a sowing for autumn and winter use. Hoe regularly.

Spinach Beet Make a sowing.

Turnips Make a further sowing once a fortnight. Thin out the seedlings regularly.

AUGUST

This is the month when crops may be harvested and when further seed sowings may be made to ensure a supply of vegetables next spring.

All the winter greens should be planted this month, and should the weather be dry, the roots may be watered in.

Broccoli If any plants of broccoli have been put out as intercrops, the main crops which they are growing in between should now be removed, and the ground between them forked over.

French Beans Harvest all the pods directly they are ready.

Runner Beans Pick regularly. Water if necessary. Mulch the rows and syringe the plants at night.

Brussels Sprouts Remove yellowing leaves. Dust regularly with derris to prevent 'blue bug' attack.

Cabbage Make further sowings of spring cabbage.

Cauliflower Go over the beds and bend a leaf over the curds so as to keep them clean and fresh.

Lettuce Further sowings may be made in a warm border. Plants previously raised may also be planted out.

Onions Autumn sown onions should be harvested after they have ripened off on the ground. Further sowings should be made for next season.

Onions, Salad Make sowings for pulling green early next year.

Peas Net rows where birds are troublesome.

Radishes Sow seeds freely.

Shallots Harvest.

Spinach Sowings may be made for winter cutting on raised beds.

Turnips Make sowings for pulling in winter.

SEPTEMBER

This is one of the biggest harvesting months, and care should be taken to get in many of the crops, especially in the case of northern gardens, as the first frost usually occurs during the last week of this month. The summer self-sown weeds may be troublesome, and hoeing should be carried out if necessary.

French Beans Look after late sown crops, and cover with cloches during the third week.

Cabbage Spring cabbage plants raised in July should now be planted in their permanent positions.

Carrots Lift and store.

Coleworts Plant out more rows.

Lettuce Sow winter varieties.

Onions Lift, ripen and store main crop varieties.

Radishes Make further sowings for autumn use.

Spinach Make final sowing. Hoe rows regularly.

Turnips Sow variety like Purple Top Milan for tops in spring.

OCTOBER

Be sure, this month to remove all dead leaves and where possible, to rot them down for manure, and clear up and burn all the rubbish in every part of the garden.

Cabbage Plant out another batch of spring cabbage.

Cauliflower Prick out plants raised in frames, 3 ins apart in cold frames.

Lettuces Plant out winter varieties sown in the seed bed in September.

Onions Store the bulbs that have ripened off on the ground.

Radishes Make another sowing.

Salsify Lift and store.

Turnips Lift the roots of the earlier sowings and store.

NOVEMBER

Every opportunity should be taken of collecting the fallen leaves during this month to put on the compost heap. This is the month when the gardener should do any digging that is deemed to be necessary.

Artichokes, Jerusalem Dig up tubers as required, or harvest and store in sand or soil.

Broad Beans A sowing may be made this month in a sheltered border, using a long-pod variety.

Broccoli Heel these over towards the north for protection and cover stems with a little soil.

Lettuce Give air to those in frames. Keep surface soil cultivated. Remove diseased bottom leaves.

Onions Examine stored bulbs. Turn over occasionally.

Parsnips Cover part of the bed with bracken or straw

so that they may be lifted in frosty weather.

Peas An attempt may be made to produce early peas next year by sowing a short row on dry soil this month.

DECEMBER

Complete all the operations commenced last month. Collect more leaves and burn only the really woody substance that is so lignified that it will not compost.

Go to the tool shed and repair and oil the tools. See that the shed is in good order. Tar and whitewash it if desired.

Store pea and bean sticks and sharpen them on wet days.

Keep a smoulder fire of wood going so as to produce good potash.

See that all the land-drains are working properly, and repair these if necessary.

Go through any inside stores of roots and remove all the decaying ones, to prevent contamination.

See that the outside clamps are thoroughly water-tight.

Broad Beans Give some protection by earthing up by bracken.

Lettuce Ventilate the frames where these are growing.

Radishes A sowing may be made in a dry, sheltered, warm south border.

Turnips Lift and store as required.

14 The importance of summer sowing for winter crops

Most people imagine that all sowing of vegetables should be made in the spring, but it is possible during June and July to sow vegetables which will give quite good crops during the autumn and winter.

To do this, the early-maturing varieties have to be chosen, and so it is like making spring sowings over again. It is very useful to be able to pull young fresh carrots in September and to gather a crop of French beans just before the autumn frosts set in.

BEETROOT

The ground should be got into a fine condition by forking and breaking, and the drills drawn out 1 ft apart. When the little plants come up and can be handled, they should be thinned out to 8 ins apart.

If the weather is hot at sowing time, the drills should be drawn out with a hoe and be thoroughly watered. This ensures quick germination – a matter of some importance.

It is a good crop to sow on land which has had a crop of autumn-sown onions on it. July sowings ensure first class roots for the autumn and winter.

Good varieties for sowing at this time of the year are: Detroit and Detroit New Globe.

CARROTS

Many people do not like the large main-crop carrots. It is said that they are too woody and dull in flavour. A supply of delicious little roots may be obtained for the autumn and winter if a sowing is made in the third week of July and another at the end of the first week in August.

Land should be used that has been well manured for a

previous crop, and it may be given a dressing of a good fish manure at 5 ozs per square yard, and, in addition, soot and wood ashes may be lightly raked in at ½ lb to the square yard.

Having raked the surface of the soil down finely, the seed should be sown in drills 1 ft apart. If sand is mixed with the seed so that it is sown thinly, there is no need to thin.

Two good varieties are Guerande Early Gem and Early Horn.

FRENCH BEANS

Sowing of French beans may be made during the first week of June and again early in July. An even later sowing than this may be made on a sunny south border towards the end of July.

When the soil is being prepared, 3 ozs of superphosphate and 2 ozs of sulphate of potash should be raked in per square yard. The rows should be 2 ft 6 ins apart, and the seed spaced out 7 ins between one another.

Good varieties for late sowing are Masterpiece and Processor.

SPINACH

Sowing of spinach may be made from the third week of June, every ten days or so, right up to the end of September. The rows should be 14 ins apart, and it is a good plan to thin the plants out when they are 2 ins high, to 4 ins apart. These thinnings may be used in the kitchen in their entirety once they have been washed.

A good variety to sow at this time of the year is Monarch Long Standing.

SPINACH BEET

Sowing of spinach beet may be made up to the last week

of August. It is a perpetual spinach, and there is no advantage in sowing it every ten days, as advised for the ordinary spinach.

Rows should be made 15 ins apart and the plants thinned out to 8 ins apart. The hoe must be kept going frequently between the rows after the plants are through, so as to encourage free growth.

The spinach should be cut regularly when it is fit to pull, the stems being removed with the leaves.

TURNIPS

Sowing of turnips can be made every fourteen days from the end of July to the beginning of September. The later sowings are often better than the earlier ones. It is astonishing how good and fresh they are.

The tops of the turnips can be used as a vegetable, as well as the roots, so such sowings provide two vegetables from one.

The drills should be 10 ins apart and the turnips thinned out to 6 ins apart. Regular dressings of old soot may be given.

When fully grown they may be lifted and stored in small clamps, as advised for potatoes. When storing, the leaves should be trimmed off, but not the tap-roots.

Good varieties are Snowball Early White Stone and Manchester Market, Early Green Top.

PEAS

Few people realise the importance of making another sowing of peas in the summer. Sowing may be made right up to the end of the first week of July. In the south good results can be had from sowing in the third week of July.

A narrow trench may be made 5 ins or so wide, and 8 ins deep. This may be filled up with good rotted compost to within 4 ins of the top of the ground, and then covered with good soil. The seed should be sown on top of this trench, in two rows 3 ins apart, the seeds being alternated or zigzagged. They should then be covered with some more soil.

See that the plants get plenty of water in dry weather, and mulch the rows with strawy manure or lawn mowings. Do not have the rows too close together, for autumn peas are subject to attacks of mildew, and in hot weather to damage by thrips. Mildew is never as bad on soil which has been enriched with potash. Wood ashes may be applied at 4 ozs to the square yard before the seed is sown.

Good varieties are Histon Mini, Meteor and Superb.

LETTUCE

Lettuce seed should be sown in small batches every three weeks from the beginning of June till the end of August. If this is done, it is possible to keep up a regular supply.

The seed should be sown in drills ½ inch deep: cabbage lettuce 9 ins apart, and cos lettuce 1 ft apart.

Lettuces will grow on almost any kind of soil, but it should be enriched with organic matter. Spent hops, horticultural sedge peat, and any other such material may be used to be *shallowly* forked in at the rate of ½ lb to the square yard or so. In addition, meat and bone meal or a good fish manure may be applied at 5 ozs per square yard.

Varieties such as advised for spring sowing may be sown now, or, if it is desired that the lettuces shall stand winter weather, such varieties as Arctic King or Imperial Winter should be sown, while with cos lettuces the best variety for winter work is Winter Density.

For this winter work the seed is usually sown either the last week in August or the second week in September. It is advisable to sow twice, as the smaller ones usually stand the winter best, and the first sowing may be rather large.

SPRING CABBAGE

This has been dealt with in Chapter 4, but, because it is so important, it is being briefly dealt with again.

The seed should be sown at the end of July and in the middle of August. If one sowing comes along too early, the other one is just right.

The seed may be sown in the rows where they are to grow, and be thinned out 6 ins apart. It is generally better to make a seed bed and sow the seed in shallow drills, 6 ins apart.

When the ground is ready for the young cabbage plants, they can be put out 18 ins by 1 ft, and any plants that are over may be left growing in the seed bed, to be used for planting up blank spaces early in the year.

Useful varieties are mentioned in Chapter 4.

ONIONS

The best time for sowing autumn onions is round about the third week of July, and it is not a bad plan to make another sowing a week or so later. The bed should be made nice and firm, and bone meal and fish manure used at 3 ozs to the square yard should be raked in.

Drills should be drawn out 10 ins apart, and the seeds sown thinly. The rows should be kept clean, but other than this the onions need little attention throughout the winter.

The best results are obtained when the rows are thinned in the spring and the thinnings are transplanted. Quite good bulbs result.

Good varieties are Ailsa Craig and White Lisbon.

For salad purposes White Lisbon is best, and is very delicious when used young. It is possible to sow this variety once a fortnight from the beginning of June up to the end of August.

15 Making the most of a small garden

The man with a small garden should do everything possible to make the most of the area at his disposal. He will get the best results if he can enrich his soil with as much organic matter as possible. The extra loads of farmyard manure, or the collection from greengrocers' shops of extra organic matter to rot down will amply repay him by the heavier crops he will produce. Once soil is brought into a good rich condition it is easily kept so. Abundant moisture is also necessary, providing the soil is well drained and in 'good heart'. Driblets of water are useless. Thorough soakings are what is necessary, and overhead sprinklings, which imitate rain, will give the best results.

He should concentrate on vegetables which take up little room and which can be sown at frequent intervals, so as to keep up a constant supply. He should make himself an expert on their culture, and though his diet will be restricted, he will be fed and his body provided with the necessary vitamins and foods.

It is suggested that he should concentrate on the following vegetables:

A stringless variety of French or kidney bean such as Processor.

Globe beet, such as Empire Globe.

Curly kale that is dense and compact, like Dwarf Green Curled.

Early-hearting spring cabbage, like Harbinger.

A variety of carrot that is practically coreless and 'turns in' quickly, like Nantes Express.

A row of chives, as an edging, for salad flavouring.

A pot leek, like Musselburgh, for the winter.

Two or three kinds of lettuce, both summer and winter.

An autumn-sown onion, like Unwins Reliance, but not

the spring-grown kinds.

A summer radish, like French Breakfast, and certainly the winter radish.

Two varieties of spinach, one a summer and the other a winter.

A globe garden turnip, like Tokyo Cross, and also a winter variety.

These vegetables should provide you with all that is necessary for the summer and winter months. A dwarf variety of pea might be included if it is specially desired, but there is not as heavy a yield of food from a row of dwarf peas as from a similar area of land devoted to some of the other crops mentioned above.

The gardener should do everything possible to intercrop and to catch-crop. Intercropping means the growing of one row of vegetables in between the rows of another, without undue detriment to either. For instance, early-maturing radishes, like French Breakfast, can be sown in between rows of perpetual spinach. A crop of lettuces can be got off between two rows of curly greens. Spinach can be sown between rows of French beans, or the French beans themselves can be sown between the rows of early-sown spinach.

A keen gardener will devise all kinds of schemes. One the author followed recently was that of planting cabbage lettuce in March, 1 ft square, and then planting some Ailsa Craig onion plants, sown the previous autumn, between the lettuces. When the lettuces were cleared, a good deal of hoeing was carried out, and then in September cabbages were planted between the onions. The onions were harvested at the beginning of October, and the cabbages the following spring, when the land was prepared for early potatoes.

Catch-cropping means the sowing of one crop immediately after the harvesting of another and before the sowing of the next main crop. Thus, if it was intended to grow French beans to be harvested in July and these were to be followed by the planting out of spring cabbage in September, some crop like spinach or lettuce could be grown between the middle of July and the second week of September with profit. Most catch-crops have to be those which are quick maturing, and the keen gardener will always have a supply of seed in hand for this purpose, or will have thought ahead and raised the necessary plants.

It is impossible in a small book of this character to go into all the possible catch-cropping and intercropping that can be done, but the man with the small garden should think of these things, and should try to get the most out of a small space.

Just one word of warning: never become so enthusiastic about intercropping that you do not give either vegetable a chance of developing properly.

16 A plan of a vegetable garden

This is the actual plan of a small vegetable garden at the end of one of those rather long narrow gardens you often find at the back of the modern houses.

It has been divided into three parts so as to be able to carry out a three-course rotation. The crops shown have been the actual crops grown in such an area of land over a period of years. The general scheme has been very successful.

Naturally the intercrops are not shown nor are the catch crops. After the potatoes, for instance, spring cabbage can be planted or spinach sown. A row of spinach can also be taken off before the peas are all sown.

The runner beans and artichokes have always been grown along the fence at the side or bottom of the garden. The seed bed $2\frac{1}{2}$ ft wide is used for the raising of plants and for growing lettuce and spinach, spring onions, corn salad, etc., later on.

Naturally, this plan will not suit every garden or every allotment. It is merely included to give a general idea as to what can be done in limited circumstances. Some may prefer to devote half the allotment to potatoes and the rest to root crops and members of the cabbage family. In this case the rotation may be said to be a two course!

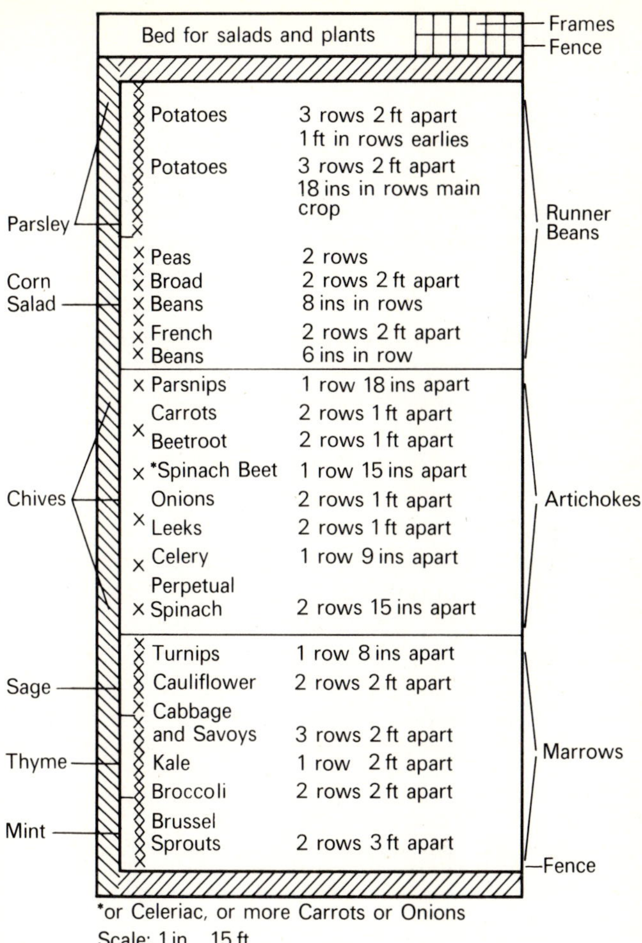

Plan of a vegetable garden. Grown runner beans, marrows trained up and Jerusalem artichokes against and along fence.

Appendix: Food values

We human beings are surrounded by synthetic foods every day. We buy jams that are dyed artificially. We are used to synthetic sweeteners. The wording often reads quite extraordinarily on packets and tins. For instance, one tin of soup contains monosodium glutamate, hydrolised protein, derivatives, colouring matter and lactic acid. A tin of chicken roll may contain rusk, hydrolised protein, monosodium glutamate, sodium nitrate and some flavouring. How many people today even read the words at all, let alone know what they mean.

The vitamin should of course be in the food you eat rather than in a pill. To be truly healthy the food you eat should be compost grown. Much depends also on how that food is cooked for to ensure the greatest value from vegetables and salads they should be eaten raw.

Grated carrots, grated heart of cabbage, lettuces, radishes, tomatoes, spring onions, parsley, cucumbers, endive and the like are delicious and full of vitamins. It is the over boiling of the cabbage, swedes, parsnips and other vegetables which does them – or you – no good.

WHAT ARE THE VITAMINS THAT ARE SO IMPORTANT AND WHAT DO THEY DO?

Vitamin A Vitamin A can easily be lost, for instance, by those who use liquid paraffin as a laxative. Using fats for frying again and again can cause factor damaging to Vitamin A as well. Even the over use of aspirin can damage the value of the Vitamin A intake. Please build up the natural Vitamin A in your body by eating watercress, spinach, dried apricots, turnip tops, carrots and fishes' roe. There is also a valuable amount in eggs, butter and cheese.

Vitamin B The Vitamin B complex is now divided up into a number of sub-sections. B1 can easily be lost in overboiling vegetables – especially when the water is thrown away. Simply toasting bread robs this food of some B1 and B2. It is Riboflavin which is found in compost grown vegetables and the record shows that it is also the vitamin which gives most protection against cancer. It is a pity really that we don't follow Sweden's example and have brown bottles for milk, as the glass bottles we use cause the Riboflavin to be lost, as well, incidentally, as Vitamin C.

To ensure the presence of this vitamin take Brewer's Yeast or yoghurt and wholemeal wheat bread – *NOT* white bread please. B6 is Pyridoxin and *compost grown* vegetables supply adequate quantities. Curiously enough bananas are rich in B6 as are peas and broad beans.

Folic acid is one of the Vitamin B's – a vitamin which is normally produced by our intestinal bacteria – but help can be given by eating fresh compost-grown green leaves of spinach, lettuce, cabbage and the like.

Vitamin C Most people know about Vitamin C, the absorbic acid vitamin, the vitamin that the government so often wrote about in the War, the 'blackcurrant vitamin' as some people call it. It was given to young people as a juice. Unfortunately, it is a vitamin that is not readily stored in the body, but is quickly dissipated in the urine.

Every member of *The Good Gardeners' Association* and every reader of this book should concentrate on giving his family fresh, compost-grown fruits and vegetables rather than tinned, processed and preserved ones. Home-grown bottled fruits are a useful addition to winter meals.

Vitamin C is found liberally in watercress, strawberries, blackcurrants, sweet peppers, raw broccoli, parsley and Brussels sprouts. It is an important vitamin for those suffering from rheumatism or with low blood pressure.

Vitamins can easily be destroyed by re-heating foods, by smoking, by adding sugar liberally to stewing fruit and by the use of saccharine and cyclamates. Fortunately the use of cyclamates has now been banned.

Vitamin D Vitamin D is important as it helps with bone and teeth formation and particularly so in the children. It does help also with fractures in adults. Sunlight on the skin helps to produce this vitamin as does the mushroom grown out of doors in the sunshine. This vitamin, like Vitamin A, is destroyed by liquid paraffin. Halibut and cod liver oil are rich in Vitamin D and so are herrings, sardines and salmon.

Vitamin E Vitamin E is an important vitamin. It is not toxic in any way and can hardly be overdone it seems, when naturally occurring. It is of course the fertility vitamin. It can be supplied by the germ of wheat, good 100 per cent wholewheat bread, the compost-grown leafy vegetables, and peanuts as well. Liquid paraffin destroys this vitamin, as do white flour and *high temperature* cookery. Vitamin E is particularly important for expectant mothers and babies, ageing men and women, and for arthritis sufferers.

Vitamin K Vitamin K is necessary for our blood and concerns coagulation. It can be found in green vegetables. The intestinal bacteria can play a great part in producing this vitamin but not if antibiotics have been taken as medicine. It is an important factor in cases of haemorrhage, because this is the vitamin that assists in the clotting.

It is therefore extremely important in the case of wounds, low blood pressure, diabetes and excessive menstrual flow.

You can receive Vitamin K by eating kales and spinach. It is also contained in tomatoes.

May I make it clear that I am not a doctor of medicine or even a nutritional expert, but I am extremely interested in growing compost food and in finding out what happens to it afterwards. This is so important for health.

What readers must realise is that when you make proper compost you are adding vitamins to the soil as well as natural antibiotics. Compost is not, as some people think, a kind of substitute for dung – it is the complete organic food for the soil. The true compost is the substance that feeds the bacteria, that makes it possible for humus to be formed and so regenerates the soil and makes it healthy. Thus a healthy soil produces healthy plants and, finally, healthy people.

Index